CONFESSIONS
OF A
SUBPRIME LENDER

CONFESSIONS
OF A
SUBPRIME LENDER

An Insider's Tale
of Greed, Fraud, and Ignorance

RICHARD BITNER

JOHN WILEY & SONS, INC.

Copyright © 2008 by Richard Bitner. All rights reserved.

Published by John Wiley & Sons, Inc., Hoboken, New Jersey.
Published simultaneously in Canada.

No part of this publication may be reproduced, stored in a retrieval system, or transmitted in any form or by any means, electronic, mechanical, photocopying, recording, scanning, or otherwise, except as permitted under Section 107 or 108 of the 1976 United States Copyright Act, without either the prior written permission of the Publisher, or authorization through payment of the appropriate per-copy fee to the Copyright Clearance Center, Inc., 222 Rosewood Drive, Danvers, MA 01923, (978) 750-8400, fax (978) 646-8600, or on the web at www.copyright.com. Requests to the Publisher for permission should be addressed to the Permissions Department, John Wiley & Sons, Inc., 111 River Street, Hoboken, NJ 07030, (201) 748-6011, fax (201) 748-6008, or online at http://www.wiley.com/go/permissions.

Limit of Liability/Disclaimer of Warranty: While the publisher and author have used their best efforts in preparing this book, they make no representations or warranties with respect to the accuracy or completeness of the contents of this book and specifically disclaim any implied warranties of merchantability or fitness for a particular purpose. No warranty may be created or extended by sales representatives or written sales materials. The advice and strategies contained herein may not be suitable for your situation. You should consult with a professional where appropriate. Neither the publisher nor author shall be liable for any loss of profit or any other commercial damages, including but not limited to special, incidental, consequential, or other damages.

For general information on our other products and services or for technical support, please contact our Customer Care Department within the United States at (800) 762-2974, outside the United States at (317) 572-3993 or fax (317) 572-4002.

Wiley also publishes its books in a variety of electronic formats. Some content that appears in print may not be available in electronic books. For more information about Wiley products, visit our web site at www.wiley.com.

Library of Congress Cataloging-in-Publication Data
Bitner, Richard.
    Confessions of a subprime lender : an insider's tale of greed, fraud, and ignorance / Richard Bitner.
        p.   cm.
    Includes index.
    ISBN 978-0-470-40219-1 (pbk.)
    1. Mortgage brokers—United States.   2. Mortgage loans—United States.
I. Title.
HG2040.B58 2008
332.7'220973—dc22

                                                                2008019035

Printed in the United States of America.

10   9   8   7   6   5   4   3   2   1

To
Deborah, Andrew, and Matthew
For always inspiring me

To Mom and Dad,
Thanks for never letting me forget
the difference between right and wrong

CONTENTS

Acknowledgments   ix

Introduction   xi

CHAPTER 1   Why I Bailed Out of the Industry   1

CHAPTER 2   The Gunslinging Business of
            Subprime Lending   15

CHAPTER 3   The Underbelly: Mortgage Brokers   39

CHAPTER 4   Making Chicken Salad Out of Chicken
            Shit: The Art of Creative Financing   73

CHAPTER 5   Wall Street and the Rating Agencies:
            Greed at Its Worst   103

CHAPTER 6   Secondary Contributors: The Fed,
            Consumers, Retail Lenders, Homebuilders,
            and Realtors   127

CHAPTER 7   How to Fix a Broken Industry   151

Glossary   183

Resources   185

ACKNOWLEDGMENTS

There are numerous people to thank for their contributions. First, my thanks to Michele Burke and Rich Trombetta, who provided critical feedback during the earliest phase of my writing and encouraged me to keep going.

I'd like to acknowledge Ryan Miller, Rob Legg, Vince Dimare, Annie Nguyen, Tres Petree, and Frank Partnoy for their contributions. I also want to thank the numerous mortgage industry professionals who provided their insights but asked not to be identified.

Lisa Gold, my editor, was instrumental in helping me work through the writing process to produce the final product. You are a gem.

To my former business partners, Mike Elliott and Ken Orman, for helping to build Kellner Mortgage Investments. You were the greatest business partners a person could have asked for.

In addition, I'd like to recognize Bob Kellner for his patience, guidance, and wisdom. Bob truly embodied the spirit that was Kellner Mortgage.

Finally, a special thanks to Ken Orman. Your willingness to help me work through the details of this story was invaluable. This book would not have been possible without your help.

INTRODUCTION

A year ago, I never thought there would be a need for me to write about the subprime industry. I knew the business was flawed, but it seemed inconceivable the events of 2007 would play out as they did. An entire segment of the lending industry has disappeared and the news gets worse by the day. Home sales have slowed, prices have fallen, credit has tightened, and the true extent of this problem, I believe, is still unknown. It has left many people wondering how bad the crisis will get.

As a 14-year veteran of the mortgage industry, five of which were spent as the owner of a Dallas-based subprime lender, Kellner Mortgage Investments, I sat front and center in the middle of this debacle. Compared to the big boys like Countrywide Financial or Washington Mutual, my firm was a small player. At our peak, we were on pace to close $250 million a year in subprime mortgages—not an inconsequential figure, but only a fraction of what the largest players were funding.

Being a lender of this size, however, afforded me a unique perspective. A typical day involved working with small mortgage brokers as well as the largest mortgage securitizers in the country. I saw the inner workings of the subprime industry from one end to the other.

Although this book is based on my experiences as a lender, it's also representative of how the entire subprime industry operated. Part of my research included interviews with numerous colleagues, many of whom worked for, managed, or owned subprime mortgage companies. I wanted to be certain that the business practices I describe were typical of the subprime industry and not isolated to my world. The insight and feedback from these colleagues were invaluable to my portrayal of the volatile mortgage business.

This is the second go-round for this book. It was originally developed as a self-published work called *Greed, Fraud & Ignorance: A Subprime Insider's Look at the Mortgage Collapse*, which I began writing in August 2007. I knew we were facing a problem of historic proportions and I felt the United States was about to experience the worst business debacle in modern history. Little did I know how right I'd be.

The problem is huge in part because so many things went wrong. First, unlike most business disasters driven by the malfeasance of a few leaders sitting at the top of the food chain, the current crisis is a result of systemic problems that extended from one end of the industry to the other. There is no single person or group who bears the greatest responsibility. Second, with 65 percent of all Americans owning a home, no other business disaster has had such a broad impact on so many people. Third, once the real estate market stops its current freefall and the gains and losses are tallied, both from the rise and fall in home equity and from losses sustained in the mortgage-backed securities market, the loss figure will reach into the trillions. Yes, trillions.

I started writing this book believing that somebody who experienced the debacle first-hand should tell the story. I quickly realized, however, that wasn't enough of a reason for writing. For me, there had to be more.

Having spent most of my business career in mortgage lending, I've generally considered myself to be an industry lifer. I want to see the mortgage industry find its moral compass and get back to the business of intelligently lending money. This can't happen without some significant changes taking place. While this book is an insider's perspective on what went wrong, the final chapter focuses on the solution. My hope that these critical changes will be made became, ultimately, my motive for writing.

Before John Wiley & Sons, Inc. entered the picture, Dan McGinn at *Newsweek* wrote an article about the earlier version of this book. Since subprime had become the newest four-letter word in the American vernacular, I knew there would be some negative reactions, but nothing prepared me for the unmitigated hatred that was directed my way. Like it or not, by putting pen to paper I had become the poster child for the subprime industry. I was guilty by association. Reading through the several hundred comments that were posted online, which recommended everything from jail time to my being drawn and quartered, I'd be lying if I said they didn't bother me. If you've been raised to believe that you should do right by others and you attempt do so on a daily basis, it's impossible not to be affected by such comments.

Let me be clear. I'm not looking for sympathy or validation. I hang my hat on the fact that during my five years as a subprime lender, my firm had an average delinquency rate of less than 3 percent. If you compare that to the current subprime delinquency rate, which hovers around 20 percent, it means my company was effective at putting borrowers into mortgage loans they could afford. That is the only criterion, in my opinion, by which a lender should be judged.

That aside, one thing is clear. Even those of us who operated with the best of intentions, and who believed in the economic benefits subprime lending had to offer, found it increasingly difficult to effectively manage risk during the last few years before the collapse. It was also difficult just to stay competitive in the marketplace. When that happens, errors in judgment take place and mistakes get made. Certainly there was no shortage in that department.

This book is about only the subprime industry, but I hope most readers will understand that the mortgage crisis is not isolated to the subprime segment of the mortgage business. Significant mistakes were also taking place with other mortgage product offerings, including those for borrowers who had good credit. They've just taken longer to show up in the delinquency reports. I discuss this more in the final chapter.

Although the book chronicles the history of my organization, *Confessions of a Subprime Lender* is not about the actions of a single person, company, or even a segment of the lending business. It's a look at how the mortgage industry collectively lost sight of its intended purpose and set off what is arguably the worst credit crisis in modern history.

CONFESSIONS
OF A
SUBPRIME LENDER

CHAPTER 1

Why I Bailed Out of the Industry

L ooking back, the idea of starting a subprime mortgage company seems crazy. That conclusion has nothing to do with the industry's implosion six years later. When we opened Kellner Mortgage Investments in September 2000, I finally realized just how little I knew about lending money to borrowers with bad credit. During the first six months in business, I felt no more qualified to pilot the Space Shuttle than to be the president of a subprime lending company.

Seven years in mortgage banking provided a solid foundation, but coming from the ranks of companies like GE Capital, my schooling was largely driven by a conservative mind-set. Lending money to borrowers with bad credit was never a part of the curriculum. When I first learned about subprime mortgages, the high-risk nature of the business made me think it was best suited for those who suffered from low morals or head trauma. Lending money to people with bad credit just seemed like a terrible idea. It wasn't until I got a taste for this business that my feelings started to change.

Taking a position as an account rep for the Residential Funding Corporation (RFC) division of GMAC in 1999 introduced me to the world of niche lending. As the largest securitizer of nonagency mortgages in the country, RFC bought loans that didn't fit the conforming guidelines of Fannie Mae and Freddie Mac. While most of the products were geared toward borrowers with good credit, RFC was just starting to make a name in subprime. It didn't take long for me to realize that buying high-risk mortgages held a lot of promise.

A few months before I took the job the subprime mortgage industry imploded for the first time, forcing most of these specialty lenders out of business. When the dust settled, RFC was one of the few survivors, which created an opportunity. My income was directly proportional to the revenue I generated, and subprime was three to five times more profitable than any other type of loan we securitized. Even though RFC gave me seven different products to sell, ranging from jumbo mortgages to home equity lines of credit, I ditched most of them in favor of subprime.

While RFC wanted us to push all their products, I saw no logical reason to sell something that made less money and carried no competitive advantage. The best way to succeed, I thought, was to take advantage of RFC's position in the subprime market.

That was the same year I met Ken Orman, the head of secondary marketing and operations for First Consolidated Mortgage Company, my best customer. It took me only a few months to realize Ken understood the business at a deeper level than most of us. He could look at a deal, size up a borrower, and immediately determine if the loan was a good risk. What impressed me most was how his gut feeling, whether or not to write a mortgage, was usually correct.

Since he was unhappy with his job and we had quickly developed a mutual respect, I saw an opening and sold him on the idea of starting our own company. Saying I was underqualified to run a subprime company isn't an exaggeration. Eighteen months at RFC introduced me to this specialty business, but it didn't prepare me for what I was about to encounter.

At RFC I bought mortgage loans that were already closed. Kellner Mortgage, our new company, was going to be a wholesale lender. We were going to target mortgage brokers, independent agents who needed help putting difficult loans together. This required a level of understanding I hadn't needed while working for RFC. Since all Kellner would look at were tough deals, the challenge was figuring out which ones were a good risk and which ones had no business getting financed. I was hoping that some of Ken's intuitive skill would rub off on me.

It's easy to lose sight of what constitutes a good credit risk when you spend all day looking at marginal deals. Fortunately, Ken taught me that the key to evaluating a loan started with asking two fundamental questions. If you can answer "yes" to both of them, he'd tell me, then you've got a subprime loan worth pursuing.

Question 1—Can the borrower afford to make the monthly mortgage payment?

Question 2—Will closing the loan put the borrower in a better position than he is in today?

At first I thought he was joking.

"That's it?" I asked him. "You've spent 10 years in subprime and your secret is asking if they can afford the payment and are they better off?"

They were simple questions but I quickly realized their true value. Being a subprime lender means living in a world of gray. Most deals aren't clear-cut and if we get bogged down in the minutiae, we'll spend all day second-guessing our own decisions. Of course, there are product guidelines to direct us, but many deals require us to make an exception. This means sound judgment, a willingness to accept risk, and the ability to trust our instincts are critical to survival. In 18 months at RFC I watched several lenders implode because they didn't possess these traits.

Fortunately, it didn't take long to get up to speed. Both Ken and our third partner, Mike Elliott, who also worked for First Consolidated

Mortgage, helped me understand the intricacies of this business. These two questions would ultimately serve as my personal reality check. Every time we doubted the logic of a specific loan, we used the questions as a litmus test. At the very least, being able to answer "yes" kept the moral compass pointing north and helped me sleep at night knowing we made the right decision.

Good Lending Gone Bad

I don't know exactly when it happened, but a few years after we opened, the business started to change. Wall Street's appetite for these loans increased at about the same time new subprime lenders entered the business. The increased competition and the red-hot real estate market led to the development of riskier products. As a lender who targeted brokers, our goal was to offer products that were similar to the competition. If we didn't keep pace with the industry leaders, we'd quickly become an afterthought. But doing this created a bigger issue. The underlying principles that governed our thinking were slowly being compromised. Answering "yes" to our questions became more difficult with each passing month.

For me the turning point came in June 2005. Until that moment, I thought we still provided a valuable service to borrowers. For all the lunacy associated with this business, I wanted to believe that writing a mortgage for borrowers still meant the odds of them making their mortgage payment were greater than the likelihood of default. Violating this basic tenet was never supposed to be part of the equation.

It wasn't until we wrote a loan for Johnny Cutter that I realized our business, the whole industry really, had lost sight of its purpose. The subprime industry, which once upon a time helped credit-challenged borrowers, was no longer contributing to the greater good. Johnny Cutter would serve as my wake-up call.

Just a good old boy from rural South Carolina, Johnny and his wife, Patti, wanted to grab a little piece of the American dream. Having picked out a newly built 1,800-square-foot house, they were relying on the same mortgage broker who worked with them in the past to secure financing.

Although we were looking at the deal for the first time, the Cutters had been down this road before. They had been turned down on two different occasions, both times as a result of bad credit. After the second decline, the broker advised them to start saving money for a down payment and work on their credit before trying again. Their credit never got better, but after three years of saving, they had enough to put 5 percent down.

The Cutters, however, bordered on deep subprime—few if any redeeming qualities. Their credit report showed they had almost no discipline when it came to managing money. With a credit score in the 500s, paying bills had never been a priority for them.

As with many subprime borrowers, the challenges didn't stop there. Since Johnny worked at a gas station and Patti was a cashier, income was tight. They would need to use more than half of their combined gross monthly income just to cover the mortgage payment. If it weren't for Patti's sister, who let them live with her for the last three years, they never could have saved any money.

Fortunately, the Cutters had two things working for them. First, they had $5,000 toward a down payment. At a time when most borrowers were trying to finance with nothing out-of-pocket, someone with a down payment was a rarity. The more money a borrower was willing to put down, the more forgiving a lender would be when it came to past credit problems. Second, the industry had been getting more aggressive with product offerings. If this deal had come through our office three years earlier it would have been declined. A poor history of paying creditors, a large number of open collection accounts, and mediocre income meant too much risk.

By 2005, the industry had a different view of the Cutters. Because of more liberal underwriting standards, they were deemed an acceptable risk. The purchase was structured so the homebuilder would pay all closing costs. The Cutters brought a cashier's check to the closing for $4,750, enough for the down payment. Three years of perseverance and some lucky timing finally paid off.

Johnny and Patti achieved their dream of being homeowners. Little did they realize just how quickly it would become a nightmare.

Watching It Crumble

Shortly after moving in, Patti was hospitalized for several days because of an illness. After missing two weeks of work to recover, she lost her job. Since Patti contributed 40 percent of the combined household income, it took a toll on their finances. She found another job but lost six weeks of income in the process.

Their biggest problem was not having medical insurance. Without coverage, Johnny used what little money he had to pay the hospital, which only covered a fraction of the total bill. The lost income and medical expenses meant something else had to give, which turned out to be the mortgage. They quickly found themselves 90 days behind with no relief in sight.

It turned out they weren't the only ones in a pickle. The investor who bought the mortgage from us issued a repurchase request. Since the Cutters didn't make their first payment, we were contractually obligated to repurchase the loan. Sometimes we could negotiate our way out or buy some time before cutting the check, but not in this case. When a borrower missed the first three payments, the loan came right back to us. To complicate matters, the Cutter loan wasn't the only deal we were being asked to repurchase. The loan repurchase requests usually came in waves, but lately they seemed to be getting worse. Depending on how hard Johnny wanted to dig in his heels, we could have been in for a long and expensive fight.

Once we bought the loan back, I called the borrowers to discuss their options. After listening to Johnny recount the events, it was hard not to feel sorry for them. They owed $25,000 in medical bills and Patti's new job paid less than her previous one. With no one to lean on for financial support, they were in a world of hurt. This couple needed a miracle, and short of some divine intervention, they were going to lose the house. The only thing left to determine was how things would play out.

"Johnny, I'm sorry to hear about your situation," I started. "As difficult as it is, we need to talk about what's going to happen next. As you know, the mortgage on your property is currently 90 days past due, which means you're $2,800 behind and your next payment is due in a week. Given your situation do you see any way possible to catch up?" I asked him.

"Well sir, I wish I could, but right now, I don't see how," he said.

From this point, one of three things could happen. First, we could start foreclosure proceedings once they were 120 days delinquent. It usually takes three to four months to complete this process. Second, the Cutters could file for bankruptcy protection. Since they were in over their heads, it would at best buy them some time and postpone the inevitable. With no money to pay the bankruptcy attorney, it was an unlikely scenario. Third, the Cutters could agree to a deed-in-lieu, which would allow them to sign the property back to us. It was the easiest way to resolve the issue, but most borrowers refuse because it requires them to move out in short order.

Johnny struck me as a straight shooter. He appeared genuine in his desire to fix the problem but he was in no position to make payments. He wouldn't say it directly, but I was sensing he just wanted a way out. If I was right, he might be willing to give us back the house.

"Johnny, if you agree to sign the deed-in-lieu, I'll do two things for you. First, I won't report it on your credit report, so no one ever has to know you gave up the property. Second, I'll let you stay in the house until the end of next month, which gives you time to find a new place to live," I said.

Considering his limited options, it was a decent offer. He would walk away from a bad situation with minimal damage, having only lost his down payment. After taking the night to think it over, he called me the next day and agreed to the offer. In the midst of his sadness, he almost sounded relieved. Faced with an impossible situation, we gave him an out and he decided to take it. He was definitely the exception. Most borrowers in this situation take the opposite approach. They'll do everything possible to avoid losing the home, right up to the point when the sheriff evicts them.

Considering we'd tied up $90,000 to repurchase the note, it felt like we had dodged a bullet. If the Cutters had filed for bankruptcy, it could have been months, maybe years, until we saw the money. We had just finished foreclosing on a property in North Carolina and it took two years to remove the borrower from that home. If a person knows how to work the system he can buy himself a lot of time.

I hated this part of the job. Being a lender is supposed to be about putting people into homes, not taking them out. I rationalized that it's just a part of the business, something every subprime lender has to go through. If only I had been able to do a better job convincing myself of that.

What Were We Thinking?

The next day I started reviewing the Cutter file. For any deal that went bad, we thoroughly reviewed the loan to find out what went wrong. Perhaps we made a mistake, or maybe the broker committed fraud. Whatever the reason, it was important to understand why the loan defaulted. Looking through the income and credit sections of the file, I wondered how the loan got approved in the first place. Here are the facts:

- The borrowers had a combined gross monthly income of $2,800.
- After paying the mortgage, they had $700 left for the month. This had to cover all their expenses—food, clothing, and everything else.
- After closing on the purchase, they had $250 left in their checking account. They had no savings or retirement accounts to fall back on. They were living paycheck to paycheck.
- Their credit was abysmal. They had no history of paying any creditor except Sears, and that account was delinquent at the

time of closing. The rest of their credit report was filled with pages of old collection and charge-off accounts.

- They had no proof of making any housing payments in the last year, since they lived with Patti's sister. We didn't know if they'd ever made a rental payment in their lives.

- In the last three years, neither of them had held a job for more than nine months at a time. Both of them had experienced significant gaps in employment.

As I went down the list, my thought was someone must have made a mistake. Aside from a good property value, there was not one redeeming factor to this loan. The credit stank, income was light, employment was spotty, and there was no rental history or savings to fall back on. Put all this together and it was a foreclosure waiting to happen. What the hell were we thinking when we closed this loan?

I checked everything in the file against the investor's guidelines, trying to figure out the mistake. Then it hit me. We did nothing wrong. Our underwriter approved the deal, we funded it, and the investor purchased it from us because it fit their guidelines. There was nothing manipulative or fraudulent about the loan. Everything from the income to the appraisal was accurate.

I was pissed off but I didn't know whom to blame. It's not as if the guidelines suddenly appeared. We'd been closing loans with similar borrower profiles for over a year. In fact, the 5 percent down payment product was a niche we'd been promoting to our brokers. For the first time I was seeing this product pushed to the extreme, and from a risk standpoint, it made no sense at all.

We'd written some pretty rough deals in the past. A few of them even made me scratch my head and wonder whether we had made a mistake. As for the Cutters, there was nothing to question. This loan didn't provide value to anyone—not to them, my company, or the investor. The Cutters caught a bad break, but for them any hiccup was going to be disastrous. With no savings and nothing to fall back on, they had no margin for error.

For all its complexity, subprime lending still comes back to our two fundamental questions. Somewhere along the way we have to believe a borrower can make the payment. The decision to lend money should require us to find something to hang our hat on, some aspect of the borrower's profile to justify the loan. It doesn't take much—income, credit, cash reserves—but something has to confirm the decision. In the end, the Cutters had nothing. This loan was indicative of an industry that had lost its way.

Time to Get Out

If the Cutters served as my wake-up call, the final alarm didn't go off until a few months later. In what I now view as more than coincidence, the same week our profit margins took a nose dive, my house, the same custom home that subprime lending helped build, caught fire. It's hard to say how the two were related, but watching the fire department battle the blaze made me realize I'd had enough. A friend reminded me it's often the dramatic events in life that provide us with clarity when we need it most. Whether it was fate or the work of a higher power, it served as the impetus I needed to make a change. The time had come to get out.

Looking back on these events made me realize just how lucky I was. No one was hurt. The fire started in the garage during the early evening, while everyone was home and awake. Since we reported it just minutes after it started, the fire department was able to get on top of it quickly, which contained the damage.

I was also fortunate to have great business partners. In the five years we owned Kellner, it was the most harmonious business relationship a person could ask for. I didn't have to tell my partners I was ready to leave, they saw it on my face. They approached me with an equitable buyout and I felt a little like Johnny Cutter. When I was stuck in a situation with no easy answers, they provided me the way out I was looking for. Like other subprime lenders, Ken and Mike hoped that order would eventually be restored to the industry. As it turned out, things would only get worse.

Friends have commented that my decision to get out before the subprime implosion took great foresight. As easy as it would be to claim that I possessed some profound wisdom and saw the implosion coming, my desire to leave was driven by the fear of losing what we had built. Looking back, I now believe my departure was a combination of luck, a desire for self-preservation, and perhaps some divine intervention.

Moving Forward

I have two reasons for writing this book. First, unless you've been totally cut off from civilization, you've read something about the subprime industry over the last year. Even with all the media coverage, there's still a more in-depth story to be told. My objective is to pull the curtain back on the subprime mortgage industry and expose it from the insider's perspective. This view will show that the niche business was built on a defective foundation.

The demise of subprime lending is a result of multiple failures. Understanding the motivations of the industry's players and how they acted in concert with each other is the key to telling this story. By exploring the brokers who originated the loans, the lenders that funded the mortgages, the investment firms that packaged them into mortgage-backed securities, and the agencies that rated the deals, we can fully understand how and where the process failed. Examining each piece in detail will show how the entire industry, from one end to the other, was at best, flawed, and at worst, negligent. The findings will also reveal the problems the housing market is currently facing are much greater than most people realize.

This book will discuss a wide variety of people and companies that operated in the world of subprime lending. As you can imagine, many of the stories don't portray them in a positive light. Real names have been used whenever possible, but in many cases they've been changed. Some of the case studies in Chapter 4 are composites drawn from dozens of typical deals. They represent the kind of activity that happened daily.

My second reason for writing this book is to develop solutions. For all its negatives and enormous imperfections, subprime lending, when used appropriately, provides value to credit-challenged borrowers. Unfortunately, industry greed has put hundreds of thousands of borrowers in jeopardy of losing their homes. Only by understanding the root cause of each problem can effective solutions be developed. When the issues are properly addressed, it's possible to have the best of both worlds—one that creates significant consumer protections but doesn't reduce the availability of credit to the marketplace.

The mortgage industry desperately needs to be fixed. The lack of investor appetite for all nonagency mortgage-backed securities has led to a massive reduction in the availability of credit. The current product offerings resemble those from 15 to 20 years ago. Until investors believe the problem has bottomed out and the issues that triggered the collapse are sufficiently addressed, borrowers will continue to suffer from reduced credit options. If we don't restore confidence in the entire lending process, from origination to securitization, the crisis will continue to grow and wreak havoc on the housing market as well as the entire economy.

CHAPTER 2

The Gunslinging Business of Subprime Lending

If you hang around the subprime lending business long enough, you'll meet your share of interesting borrowers: strippers, cons, pimps, thugs, and various other upstanding citizens of the community. These were not our typical customers. But if a borrower has credit problems and a checkered past, employment gaps, or income from unverifiable sources, he usually ends up talking with a subprime lender. Strangely enough during my five years at Kellner Mortgage, loans to borrowers who worked as ministers had one of the highest fraud rates of any profession.

Since my company, Kellner Mortgage Investments, was a wholesale mortgage company, we didn't deal directly with borrowers. We funded loans to subprime borrowers who were brought to us by mortgage brokers. The broker's job was to convince us to fund their client's loan. Inevitably, the brokers seemed to start the conversation with us by always using the same four words, "I got a guy . . ." Listening to their lengthy explanations of why their borrowers were not responsible for their current predicament, and thus somehow worthy of financing, made for an interesting case study in the art of persuasion.

When Angelo, one of our regular brokers from south Texas, called Ken about funding a potential loan, the key was looking past Angelo's b.s. and getting to the facts.

"Hey Ken, it's Angelo. You got a second?"

"Sure," Ken says.

"Cool. Let me tell you about this deal. I got a guy. He's a great dude but he's really had some bad luck. His name is Rock Gonzalez."

Translation: "A great dude" meant that Angelo would vouch for his character. This meant nothing since Angelo was less than punctual when it came to paying his own bills. "Bad luck" could mean anything, but in this case the borrower had trouble holding on to a job for more than 6 to 12 months. Angelo faxed over the loan application and credit report for prequalification, and Ken determined the loan was a run-of-the mill deal: Rock had barely okay credit, but still qualified for a mortgage with no money down. We approved the loan, and 30 days later the deal closed. That's when things started to go sideways.

Keep in mind that we knew none of the following information before funding the loan; everything during the due diligence process was either misrepresented or not disclosed.

It turns out that Rock, an ex-con, operated a business with the seller of the property, Cindy, who was also his girlfriend. He maintained a separate apartment but spent most of his time living in her home, the same house he was trying to purchase. They had two objectives for conducting the transaction. Cindy was two months behind on her mortgage and desperately needed to catch up. They also wanted to infuse some cash into their business. Although Cindy had built up a little equity in her home, she wasn't able to refinance because of her poor credit. By selling the home to Rock, she could pay off the mortgage, get some cash, and her problems would be solved. If only life were that simple.

Angelo had known Rock for several years having met him at the local gentlemen's club. What Rock didn't know was that Angelo had a thing for Cindy but just couldn't get up the nerve to tell anybody. Occasionally, Angelo and Cindy would mildly flirt with each other, but Cindy tended to flirt with everybody. After a while, Angelo made himself believe that she felt the same way about him as he did about her. That was a big mistake.

Once the loan finally closed, he decided to make his move. When Cindy refused his advances, Angelo was stunned. He went home and proceeded to drink himself into a stupor. The more he drank, the angrier he became. Finally, he picked up the phone and called Cindy, threatening her life.

When Cindy told Rock what happened, he shrugged it off. He thought that Angelo was harmless. But when Rock jokingly suggested Cindy should go out with Angelo, Cindy went crazy. She grabbed a baseball bat and started taking swings at his head. Rock bolted from the house. According to Rock, Cindy threatened to "cut off his nuts if he ever set foot in the house again."

Keep in mind that Cindy was no longer the owner of the property, which created an interesting shift. With Rock not living in the house that he had just purchased, he quickly lost the motivation to make the mortgage payment—leaving Kellner stuck with a fraudulent, nonperforming loan.

While this scenario was playing out, we'd already sold the loan to our investor, who promptly required us to buy it back. We had to threaten to report Angelo, Rock, and Cindy to the Texas Attorney General's office before we could get any cooperation from them, but we eventually worked out of the mess after Rock sold the property and the loan was paid off.

Angelo later called Ken in our office one afternoon, drunker than a skunk, promising to make it up to him for getting us in trouble with our investor. He never did. Of course, given how drunk he was at the time, it's unlikely he would have remembered ever making the phone call.

This deal had a little bit of everything: the broker misrepresenting the borrower, the borrower misrepresenting himself, the seller misrepresenting herself, a fraudulent loan application, a misrepresented appraisal, a falsified verification of employment. It was more extreme than the typical fraudulent loan, but it was typical of the type of transaction that tended to walk through our door.

I graduated from an Ivy League university believing that one day I would swing for the fences and make it to the big leagues of corporate finance. This loan made me realize that somewhere along the way I'd made a wrong turn. As a subprime lender, I felt more like I was playing in the bush leagues.

The Business of Subprime Lending

Since the current housing fiasco is tied directly to the subprime industry, it's easy to believe that lending money to borrowers with damaged credit is a bad idea. One newspaper columnist argued that financing subprime borrowers should never have been allowed in the first place. It's an understandable reaction given the rising number of foreclosures, but a closer look at the performance of subprime loans supports a different viewpoint.

Even though mortgage delinquencies are hitting record highs, the vast majority of subprime borrowers are making timely mortgage payments. Admittedly, overall delinquencies are far too high, but the fact that most borrowers are making payments means that lending money to credit-challenged borrowers is not a totally flawed proposition. The issues we're currently facing are a function of a much deeper problem—one that goes to the heart of how the industry operated.

To understand subprime lending, we must explore the mechanics of the industry—how and why it functioned as it did. The rest of this chapter will describe the profile of the subprime borrower, trace the evolution of subprime lending from its beginnings in the 1980s through its first crisis in the 1990s, examine the players and their motivations, and explain the unique subculture of the industry. Once this foundation has been established, we can examine the business in greater detail.

Subprime Borrowers and Credit Scores

Subprime borrowers are unable to qualify for conventional or conforming mortgages because they have less than perfect credit, usually because they've made late payments or defaulted on previous debt. These borrowers pay a higher interest rate and loan fees to offset the increased risk.

Borrowers can be classified as subprime because of income or employment issues, but the main reason is usually damaged credit. The most important part of a borrower's credit profile is the credit score. Understanding what it means and how it's used is vital to developing a customer profile.

A credit score is a measure of a person's credit risk, calculated using the information from their credit report. These scores, which range from 300 to 850, are compiled by credit bureaus, companies that collect and sell information about each person's credit worthiness. The three largest credit bureaus in the United States are Equifax, TransUnion, and Experian.

Credit scores are commonly referred to as FICO scores, which is an acronym for the Fair Isaac Corporation. A FICO score is a specific credit score issued by the Experian credit bureau. Equifax and TransUnion also used Fair Isaac to develop their own proprietary scoring models. Although a borrower has only one true FICO score, the acronym is commonly used as the generic term for credit score.

Borrowers with scores above 620 are classified as conforming (they conform to Fannie Mae or Freddie Mac guidelines) or Alt-A. Both require good credit, but Alt-A loans have other variables, such as a borrower who qualifies without having to prove income. Subprime borrowers have credit scores from 500 to 620; potential borrowers with scores below 500 are unable to qualify.

Though credit scores largely determine the loan type, there are exceptions. A borrower with a 640 credit score and a recently discharged bankruptcy might be considered subprime, while a borrower with a 580 credit score and compensating factors could qualify for a conforming mortgage. Chapter 4 explores the subject of credit in greater detail.

Types of Subprime Borrowers

There are no official definitions for what constitutes a subprime borrower, but most can be described in one of four ways:

1. *Slow to Pay.* These individuals have a history of paying their creditors late. This category represents the bulk of all subprime borrowers.
2. *Underqualified.* These consumers have little credit history, so they're unable to earn a good credit score. Many borrowers don't realize until they apply for a mortgage that having little or no credit can be worse than having poor credit.
3. *Life Challenged.* Borrowers who face a traumatic event, such as a divorce, failed business, or medical problem, can experience income or credit challenges as a result. This can prevent them from getting a low interest rate.
4. *Unlucky.* This can describe two types of borrowers. The first are those who are not habitual credit abusers, but whose credit score has dropped because of an unusual circumstance (such as forgetting to pay bills while away). The second are borrowers whose credit is on the cusp between conforming and subprime. If they choose the right broker or lender (someone looking out for their best interest), they qualify for a conforming rate. But if they choose the wrong person, they get a subprime mortgage.

Until 1998, home prices and income increased in relative proportion to each other, which meant housing affordability remained largely unchanged. Over the next 10 years, the balance between the two became skewed. While income grew marginally, home prices skyrocketed, which created an affordability gap. With more homebuyers struggling to qualify, a new type of subprime borrower emerged:

High Risk. These borrowers faced two challenges in purchasing a home: no down payment, and not enough income to qualify. The development of new subprime loan products to serve the needs of these borrowers greatly contributed to the industry's demise.

The Evolution of Subprime Lending

Subprime lending has no official start date, but three events paved the way for the industry's formation.

- The Depository Institutions Deregulation and Money Control Act (DIDMCA) of 1980 made the subprime business legal by allowing lenders to charge higher rates and fees to borrowers.
- The Alternative Mortgage Transaction Parity Act (AMPTA) of 1982 allowed the use of variable interest rates (ARMs) and balloon payments.
- The Tax Reform Act (TRA) of 1986 prohibited the deduction of interest for consumer loans but allowed it for mortgages on a primary residence, increasing the demand for mortgage debt. When deductibility was factored in, even high-cost mortgage debt was a better option than consumer debt.

Although these changes helped launch the industry, two market-driven events contributed to the initial growth phase. First, by late 1993, the industry was coming to the end of a refinance cycle. With interest rates going up, loan volume in the conforming market was shrinking. To fill the void, brokers and lenders began originating subprime mortgages.

Second, Wall Street investment firms began securitizing these mortgages. Securitization is a process where thousands of mortgage loans are bundled together into financial products called mortgage-backed securities (MBSs). These investments are secured by the principal and interest payments made by consumers. The process, which already existed for conforming and Alt-A mortgages, created an end or secondary market for the product.

While working at RFC, I bought subprime loans from Tony DeLuca, viewed by many as the first subprime mortgage company in Texas. He explains the impact that securitization had on the subprime market.

> When I started in 1989, there was no secondary market for these loans, which meant I had to use a private investor. Since our investor paid us nothing for the loans, the only profit we made came from the fee we charged the borrower.
>
> In 1993, my investor ran into a problem, which forced me to find another source. The next day I went searching online and found a company called Equicon that wanted to buy my loans. They came to my office, underwrote the loan files, and paid me a premium for the first time. This redefined the business. Overnight, we went from having to charge the borrower to make a profit, to paying brokers a premium the way the industry does today.

The process of packaging mortgages into securities turned these illiquid assets that could not be easily sold into liquid ones. With a secondary market to trade them in, investors quickly developed an appetite for buying these high-yield securities. The increased demand meant companies like Equicon paid lenders a premium to acquire them.

The Economics of the Business

As the appetite grew for these securities, so did the price to purchase the mortgages. By 1994, investors were paying upwards of 700 basis points (bps) per loan, or 7 percent of the loan amount.

Even a small company had enormous profit potential: A total monthly volume of $10 million, multiplied by 7 percent (700 bps), would result in a gross profit of $700,000. With 300 bps ($300,000) in total costs, a subprime lender could earn $400,000 in monthly net revenue. To be able to produce this income with fewer than 50 employees was phenomenal.

To feed the increased demand for the securities, investors began to relax the underwriting guidelines, which enabled lenders to extend financing to more credit-challenged borrowers. Tony DeLuca describes the events that repeated themselves a decade later.

> By the mid-90s, investors really got an appetite for subprime and started getting aggressive with what they bought. For a while, ContiMortgage, my main investor, was buying every mortgage we showed them, even the loans that didn't fit their matrix. It didn't matter how rough the loan was, they always bought the loan. After a while we started to joke their program guidelines were more like suggestions since the underwriters didn't follow them anyway.

The First Crisis—1998

In 1998 Long Term Capital Management (LTCM), the well-known hedge fund of Salomon Brothers bond trader John Meriwether and Nobel Prize–winning economists Myron Scholes and Robert Merton, ran into problems. Like many hedge funds, they based their investment strategy on a mix of foreign bonds and currencies. While the strategy forged by the economists was rather complex, it didn't take into consideration that a market could behave irrationally. When Russia looked like it would default on its debt, a crisis ensued.

Because the investments were highly leveraged, the fund quickly lost half its value. With a large number of banks and pension funds invested in LTCM, the impact was significant. There was serious concern at the time about whether the problems could bankrupt these institutions. In a bold move, Federal Reserve Chairman Alan Greenspan convinced the banks to remain in the fund, which averted disaster. By lowering the Fed Funds rate, the interest rate banks charge each other for overnight loans, he also sent a powerful message: The Fed would take whatever action was necessary to avoid catastrophe.

With investors retreating to safer investments, the secondary market for subprime mortgages dried up. When fewer investors were willing to purchase these loans, the industry experienced a major shakeout. Many of the top 25 players quickly went out of business, and the rest either merged or failed shortly afterward.

While the 1998 crisis has similarities with the current one, there are some differences. John Mauldin, President of Millennium Wave Advisors, made an excellent comparison in his August 11, 2007, article, "Back to the 1998 Crisis, Subprime to Impact for a Long Time."

> In 1998, problems in Asia and Russia spread to the rest of the markets, affecting US stocks. It took a few months to sort out, and a lot of people lost money. Today, problems in the subprime mortgage markets spread to other credit markets and the effect is spilling over into the stock markets. But there is a difference. Today, instead of one fund that was the epicenter of the problem, the problems are spread around among scores of funds and permeate the largest institutional and pensions funds. While that means the losses are spread among thousand of investors, it also means that central banks can't bring everyone to the table to fix the problem. . . . And one last difference between 1998 and today. Back then, the problems in the market became known and were priced into the markets in relatively short order. It's going to be several years before we know the extent of the subprime losses.

With many investors having lost their appetite for high-risk mortgages, the market experienced a major pricing correction. Overnight, lenders went from making 700 basis points down to 300 to 400. As months passed and the market stabilized, prices eventually leveled at 500 bps. For those lenders who survived the crisis, subprime lending still remained a viable business opportunity.

Understanding the Players and the Process

To understand mortgage lending, you must know the players, their roles, and their motivations. Figure 2.1, the mortgage industry "food chain," breaks down the lending process by identifying the industry segments and their functions with arrows showing the path a mortgage follows.

When consumers need a mortgage, they can use either a mortgage broker or a mortgage lender/banker. Brokers only originate the mortgages, while lenders close the loans in their own name, using their own funds.

Since loans must be securitized in large quantities, most lenders like Kellner Mortgage rely on bigger lenders, companies like GMAC and Countrywide, to purchase loans from them. In turn, these companies aggregate the mortgages from numerous sources before securitizing them. Since we sold loans directly to these larger lenders, I'll refer to them as investors throughout the book.

What happens next depends on the type of loan. If the loan is a conforming or prime loan, it gets sold to Fannie Mae or Freddie Mac. These government-sponsored entities (GSEs) package the loans into mortgage-backed securities (MBSs). If the mortgages don't meet the guidelines established by the GSEs, lenders use investment firms to package them into nonagency MBSs. Excluding home equity loans, there are three types of nonagency MBSs: Jumbo A, Alt-A, or Subprime. The institutions that purchase the MBSs range from hedge and pension funds to foreign investors. The sale of these securities is dependent on the rating agencies, companies like Moody's and Standard and Poor's. They provide judgments about whether these investments will pay interest on schedule until they mature. They rate the securities with a letter grade (AAA to BB–) to indicate the level of risk associated with the investments. Since

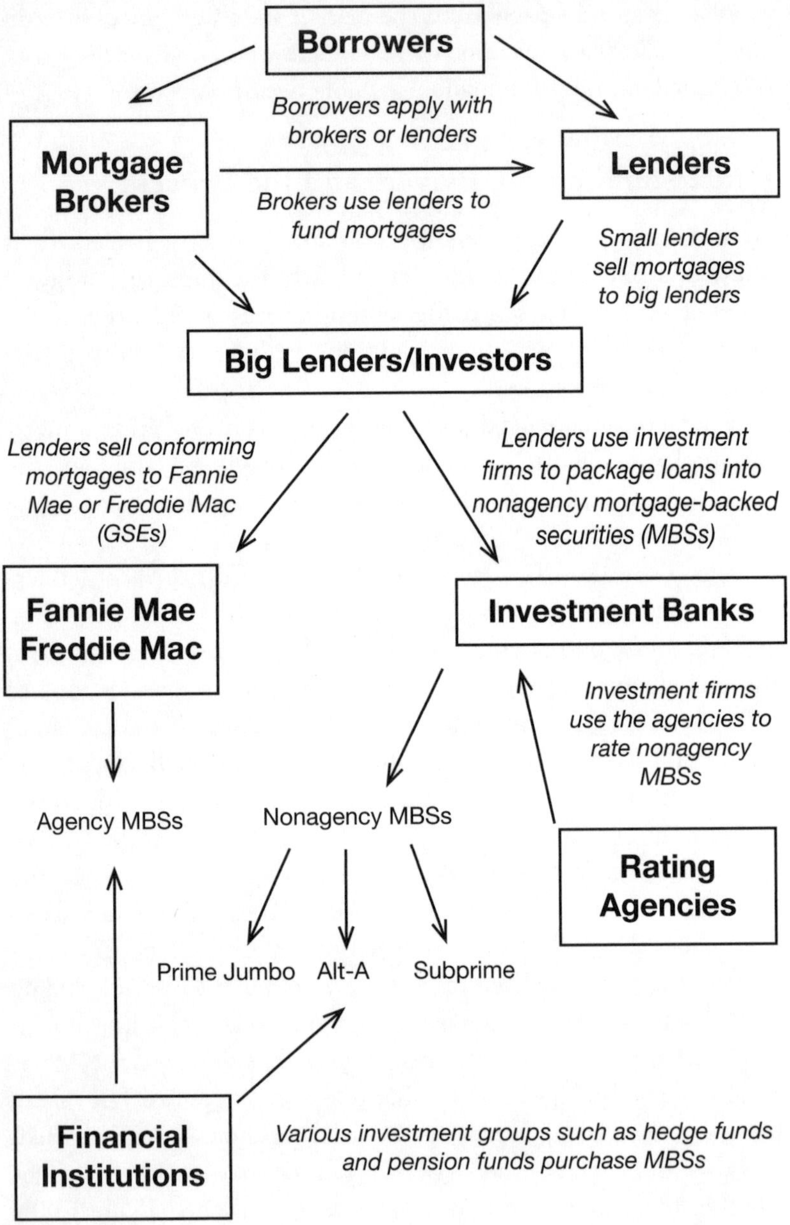

Borrowers

Borrowers apply with
brokers or lenders

**Mortgage
Brokers**

Brokers use lenders to
fund mortgages

Lenders

Small lenders
sell mortgages
to big lenders

Big Lenders/Investors

Lenders sell conforming
mortgages to Fannie
Mae or Freddie Mac
(GSEs)

Lenders use investment
firms to package loans into
nonagency mortgage-backed
securities (MBSs)

**Fannie Mae
Freddie Mac**

Investment Banks

Investment firms
use the agencies to
rate nonagency
MBSs

Agency MBSs   Nonagency MBSs

**Rating
Agencies**

Prime Jumbo   Alt-A   Subprime

**Financial
Institutions**

Various investment groups such as hedge funds
and pension funds purchase MBSs

Figure 2.1   Mortgage Industry Food Chain

this book focuses on the subprime industry, government loans (FHA and VA) have been excluded from the chart.

Lender-Broker Relationship

The business of brokering mortgage loans is subject to controversy. As independent agents, brokers don't work for the lender, nor do they represent the borrower. They provide the borrower with a service, but the two have no legal agreement. Depending on the circumstances, the broker might get paid by the consumer, lender, or both. So, to whom do they have a fiduciary duty? The answer is unclear, which creates the potential for abuse. Since neither the industry nor the government has adequately addressed the issue, the broker is left to determine what constitutes appropriate behavior.

Unfortunately, most broker-lender agreements provide little clarity on the subject. Instead they focus on the main concern for all subprime lenders—fraud. With hundreds of millions of dollars in transactions occurring daily, one rogue broker can inflict tremendous damage on a lender. Because of the risk, lenders require brokers to repurchase a mortgage if it's found to be fraudulent. The challenge, however, comes with enforcement. There are two issues to consider.

1. A lender may suspect a broker of committing fraud, but proving it is often difficult. As you'll see in Chapter 3, fraud can often be subtle, making it hard to spot. Even when a suspicious act is detected, the lender will ask who is responsible, the consumer or the broker. If the broker is guilty, the lender will inactivate his account. When the answer is unclear, the lender has to make a judgment call. Unless the lender sustains a financial loss as a direct result of a broker's actions, the broker has little to lose by acting recklessly. Even for the worst violators, lenders must still use the courts to obtain any financial relief.

2. Brokers seldom have the ability to repurchase a loan. Most of them are small companies with little cash. A broker with a

net worth of $50,000 (which is high for the average broker) can't buy back a $250,000 loan. It's difficult to recover any money from brokers, which makes litigation a costly and unappealing alternative. Unfortunately, when lenders don't pursue legal action, brokers are left to inflict damage on other mortgage bankers.

Lender-Investor Relationship

Historically, the investors who purchase subprime mortgages from companies like Kellner have been large lenders, banks, or financial institutions such as Countrywide or HSBC. This group would eventually include the Wall Street investment firms such as Merrill Lynch or Bear Stearns.

These investors set the tone for the market. Their tolerance for risk and what they can securitize will determine the products they offer. In turn, the products are made available to lenders, who offer them to brokers and ultimately the consumer. As a small lender, my company partnered with four investors: GMAC Residential Funding (RFC), Countrywide, HSBC, and Citi. Most subprime lenders partnered with several investors to provide multiple outlets for selling mortgages.

Any institution that either funds or purchases a mortgage has a financial interest in its performance. For lenders and investors, there are three areas of mutual concern: prepayment speeds/premium recapture, early payment default, and loan repurchase due to fraud.

1. *Prepayment Speed/Premium Recapture.* When a mortgage pays off (prepays) through a home sale or a refinance, this asset no longer exists. If loans are prepaying faster than expected, the performance of the mortgage-backed security is negatively impacted, which means investors make less money.

Since subprime borrowers are charged higher interest rates, investors are concerned with how fast loans will prepay. If a borrower closed on a mortgage and then improved his credit, he could refinance at a better rate. If his loan prepays within the first year, the lender is required to pay back a portion of the premium paid by the investor, which is called premium recapture. To mitigate this risk, lenders attach prepayment penalties to mortgages whenever possible.

Lending money to people with bad credit is a risky proposition. The subprime business model only made sense if borrowers kept the mortgage and made payments for at least a few years. The use of prepayment penalties helped the industry create a deterrent against accelerated loan payoffs.

Until states and consumer activist groups began to address the issue, investors paid a greater premium for loans that carried longer prepayment penalties. I attended a client event sponsored by HSBC in 2003 and listened to the head of trading discuss their pricing model. He confirmed in great detail what we had been seeing for some time. Most investors built their pricing models around the sweet spot, the two-year adjustable mortgage with a three-year prepayment penalty, because it maximized revenue for everyone in the food chain.

Unfortunately this model also handcuffed the consumer. When the interest rate was set to adjust after two years, a borrower trying to refinance faced some unpleasant choices: pay a stiff penalty (as much as 5 percent of the loan amount), or make higher payments for the next year. If the borrower had little equity in the property, it meant he was stuck with the loan until the penalty expired.

2. *Early Payment Default (EPD)*. In most cases, lenders are contractually obligated to repurchase a loan they've sold to an investor in the event of an early payment default (when a borrower doesn't make the first payment to the investor). Although this was the industry standard, it varied between investors. At one end of the continuum was GMAC Residential Funding (RFC), who had no EPD requirement. On the other end was Countrywide, who required a loan to be repurchased if the borrower either missed the first payment or became 90 days delinquent within the first year.

3. *Loan Repurchase (Fraud)*. If a loan isn't considered an early payment default but still becomes delinquent at some point in the

future, investors perform a quality control review to search for any sign of impropriety. When a loan experiences problems, the investor is looking for any reason to have a lender repurchase it. Unlike brokers, most lenders have the financial capacity to repurchase loans. When a broker commits fraud, the lender must prove it in order to make the broker buy it back. The investor, however, only needs proof that fraud occurred—who committed the act is largely irrelevant. Because of this threat, lenders have little motive to act in a fraudulent manner. However, as Chapter 4 illustrates, it doesn't mean they can't get creative.

A Conflicted System

When you consider the motives for all three players—brokers, lenders, and investors—the mortgage food chain presents a system in conflict. Lenders are sandwiched between two groups with completely different agendas. On one hand, they answer to investors who care about loan performance and prepayment speeds. If a lender's book of business performs poorly, the investor can terminate the relationship. Therefore, lenders want the performance of their loans to meet the investor's expectations. On the other hand, lenders cater to brokers, a group whose only motivation is closing the loan. Since brokers have no financial interest in a loan's performance and face no liability, lenders must always question their actions and motives.

A Culture All Its Own

Until a few years ago, most lenders fit into one of two categories—those who handled subprime mortgages and those who didn't. Since subprime involved taking on more risk, it also required a different mind-set and willingness to operate under a different system.

The first difference was the need for more capital. Unless a lender is a bank, it seldom uses its own money to fund mortgages. Instead, most lenders use warehouse lines of credit as their source of capital. A warehouse lender holds or stores the note until an investor purchases the loan. It's like a giant secured credit card, with the note to the property serving as collateral.

The advance rate, the percentage of the loan amount the warehouse lender will provide to fund a loan, has traditionally been higher for prime than for subprime loans. In the 1990s, a prime lender might get a 99 percent advance rate, meaning the warehouse lender advances 99 percent of the loan amount with the lender contributing the other 1 percent. A subprime lender might get a 98 percent advance rate, which requires twice as much capital to invest as a prime lender. Funding $10 million in monthly volume requires $200,000 ($10 million × 2%) in capital just to fund the loans. That's a large capital requirement, and it doesn't include the money needed to run the rest of the operation.

The second difference came from not knowing if investors would buy the loans. Conforming lenders benefited from the use of automated underwriting programs developed by Fannie Mae and Freddie Mac. An approval through one of these systems all but guaranteed an investor would purchase the loan.

By 2000, automated underwriting was just being developed for subprime mortgages. This meant underwriting a loan file was a risky proposition, one that could prove costly. If a lender made a mistake or if the investor's underwriter declined the loan after it had been closed, they had to find another outlet. That usually meant selling the loan at a loss on the "scratch and dent" market, where lenders go to sell loans their investors won't purchase.

If your vision of mortgage lending is one of high finance with suits and ties, then you're thinking of the prime side. Subprime lending was more of a jeans and t-shirts crowd. Many of the earliest subprime employees got their start in the consumer finance industry at companies like Beneficial, Conseco, and The Associates. Since these companies lent money to people with poor credit, subprime mortgages were a natural transition.

If anyone fit the stereotypical profile of a subprime lender, it was Tony DeLuca. Standing over 6'6", Tony, with his goatee, large physical presence, and a deep voice that would have made James Earl Jones envious, looked intimidating. If he hadn't been a subprime lender, he would have made a great collection agent.

For me, dealing with Tony was a challenge. Coming from the prime side of the industry, I was used to customers with low-key personalities. With Tony, most transactions were a struggle—either our price was too low or our underwriters were too conservative. Even when deals went smoothly, there was a palpable tension that made doing business a painful process.

Even though Tony could be difficult, his loans performed well. After 10 years of running a subprime mortgage company, he understood how to manage risk. I pushed hard to get his business and Tony quickly became my second-best customer. Even though he represented 20 percent of my total business, his hardened approach eventually wore me down.

After an especially difficult transaction, I finally had enough. When he picked up the phone, I went after him. "Tony, it's Richard. We need to have a conversation. Actually, let me rephrase that. For the next 30 seconds, I'm going to talk and you're going to listen. This relationship is becoming a complete and total ass-whip. No matter what we do, you end up treating us like shit. So here's what's going to happen. Starting right now, you're either going to begin acting civil to everyone on my team or we're done."

It was a risky move considering that Tony could have told me to go to hell. Even though the recent correction had significantly reduced the number of subprime investors, GMAC Residential Funding (RFC) wasn't the only game in town. He could have gone somewhere else.

Tony fired back at me, "Well then, I guess I'm going to have to get a new RFC rep."

"No Tony, you don't seem to understand something," I interrupted. "I'm your only option. There are no other reps available for you. You either play nice, work with me, or this relationship is finished."

The most important part of running a convincing bluff is knowing what cards your opponent is holding. I had no intention of cutting him off, but something had to change if this relationship was going to work. Tony could use other investors, but I knew he was very selective about whom he sold to. He disliked having to bring new companies into the mix and I was counting on that to work in my favor.

Looking back, the whole conversation must have taken him by surprise. Because of his booming voice and physical presence, most people had no desire to go toe-to-toe with him. I believe it might have been the first time a vendor tried to back him into a corner. Fortunately, his tone changed. Instead of fighting back, he admitted that he occasionally acted abruptly and let his emotions get the best of him. He went on to explain that even his wife told him he could be gruff at times. I was thinking of a different word but left it at that.

Ultimately, the conversation paid several dividends. Standing up to Tony not only helped us to become friends, it taught me something about myself. I already knew that being a subprime lender required a high tolerance for risk, a willingness to get your hands dirty, and thick skin. I now knew just how thick my own skin was.

The most interesting part about the subprime business was the people, some of whom were very colorful. As a business owner, the challenge was figuring out who you could trust and who was a scoundrel in disguise. Although my five years in the business were filled with numerous stories, some of the most interesting discoveries continue to unfold to this day, more than two years after I left the company.

Shortly after opening Kellner, we used a warehouse line of credit through nBank, a Georgia-based lender. Our contact, Ron Walton, came across as a true southern gentlemen—very professional in his approach. We used his company for only eight months, but our dealings led us to believe he ran a good, clean operation. I only recently discovered just how wrong we were.

In August 2007, Walton was sentenced to 97 months in federal prison and ordered to pay restitution for using his position at the bank to facilitate a fraud scheme with several mortgage brokers.

Even though he had several co-conspirators, he is credited with putting this 103-year-old Georgia bank out of business.

Whether it was the lure of higher profit margins or the risky nature of the business, something about the subprime industry attracted a different crowd. While some individuals were more reckless than others, almost fearless, I viewed many of them as gunslingers. It would ultimately take someone with a gunslinger mentality to help launch our company.

How to Start a Subprime Company with No Money Down

For us, starting a mortgage company seemed like a long shot. In 2000, most subprime investors required lenders to have a net worth that ranged from $250,000 to $500,000. It was a small number by industry standards, but for the collective partners at Kellner Mortgage, it was far more than we could afford. We didn't lack desire or ambition, just capital.

But having worked in subprime lending for 18 months, I understood a few things about the business. If you make a sales pitch to enough people and sound convincing in the process, you'll find someone willing to take a risk, even if it makes little sense. The birth of our company would depend on it.

We came up with an idea to start off as a branch office under an existing subprime lender. In our proposal we asked for total access to the lender's warehouse lines and investors, along with complete underwriting authority. Not surprisingly, no one we pitched this proposal to was willing to back it. Their reluctance was understandable, since we wanted total control. Despite all the risks in this business, we asked for a lot. It would take little effort to inflict major damage on another lender's operation. Whoever took this deal would need to be more than a gunslinger—they'd need to have an exceptionally high tolerance for risk.

Luckily, one of my customers saw something he liked and went after it. Randy Gomez, owner of American Fidelity Mortgage, put us in business. Of course, the price of admission wasn't cheap—it cost us 25 percent of gross revenue and 12 percent interest for an unsecured line of credit, just so we could operate.

Fortunately our timing was perfect. By early 2001, we had a small staff of 12 employees. The Fed was cutting rates, volume was beginning to increase, and things were looking up. At the same time, Gomez's offices were also growing, which created a problem. Earlier in this chapter we discussed how lenders use warehouse lines of credit to fund mortgages. Like a credit card, when the line is maxed out, loans must be sold to investors to make room for new ones. With Gomez scrambling to acquire new warehouse lines, we didn't have enough space on the existing lines to fund the loans.

For weeks, borrowers closed on their loans and were forced to wait for days for the funds to arrive. Customers were furious and the situation was getting desperate. We could only operate this way for so long until brokers would pull their loans and go somewhere else. The following morning, my partners and I decided to take control of our future.

In a desperate move, I convinced my parents to mortgage their house to capitalize the company. With the profit made during our first six months, we had enough cash to run the business, but needed to show money on the audited financial statements to get our investor approvals. Having secured the necessary funding, we formed our own company and made a break.

We started the company with a total net worth of $414,000, still short of the $500,000 many investors required. Fortunately, we were able to leverage the relationships we built selling loans under the American Fidelity umbrella to get our approvals. We also benefited from incredible timing—had we tried this idea two years later it would have failed. By 2003, most investors had raised the minimum net worth requirement for lenders to $1 million, an amount we couldn't obtain.

The biggest challenge came with getting our Countrywide approval. At the time, Countrywide required all wholesale lenders to have a minimum net worth of $3 million. With only $414,000 on our audited balance sheet, asking for the exception seemed laughable. As a start-up with 12 employees closing less than $5 million per month, there was no justifiable reason for them to approve us.

I spent 45 minutes with their analyst trying to convince her that declining our application would be the single greatest mistake in the 35-year history of their company. It's difficult to remember all the bullshit nonsense I slung during that phone call, but I'm fairly certain it included some delusional argument about Kellner and Countrywide working together to house America. I'm still not certain how it happened, whether it was great timing, sheer luck, or pure moxie, but they bought the argument and waived the requirement.

That's when I started thinking, maybe there is a little gunslinger in me after all.

CHAPTER 3

The Underbelly: Mortgage Brokers

In mid-2007, I received an e-mail that summed up the insanity that had infiltrated mortgage finance. The message was simply a photo of a business sign hung in front of an office. It read:

Welcome to U S Center
Hair, Nails

Mortgages

Apparently the advertisers wanted to cash in on the housing boom along with everyone else. Comical as it was, the sign illustrated just how much the mortgage business had grown. If beauticians were offering mortgages, who might be next? During a plane flight in 2005, a former employee of mine sat next to a pilot traveling on vacation. He informed her he had just gotten a broker's license and was planning to leave his job and work full-time as a loan officer.* I hope he didn't give up his day job.

By 2004, brokers were entering the business in droves. With so many new brokers wanting to get approval to do business with Kellner, we had to hire more employees to process the applications. According to Wholesale Access, a residential lending market researcher, the industry peaked at 53,000 mortgage broker companies in 2006, nearly a 50 percent increase from the 2001 figure of 37,000. By some estimates, the number of new loan originators working for mortgage brokers increased by 100,000 during this period.

Annie Nguyen was our first loan coordinator and eventually managed the entire department. As the go-between for the broker and the underwriter, she and her team of coordinators helped the mortgage brokers we worked with make sure all the loan conditions were met. This put her in close contact with our customers, the brokers. Here are her thoughts on the state of the business at that time.

> After a while, things just got crazy. My employees told me stories of brokers who didn't know anything about the business. We'd receive loan files where the loan applications were blank and the disclosures were incorrect or missing. For many loans we had to go hunting for the information.
>
> I once had a loan officer ask me if we really needed to have an appraisal before closing. I thought he was joking. He didn't understand why he couldn't get it to us after the loan had funded. We spent so much time doing quality control we went from being loan coordinators to full-time fraud detectors.

---

*A quick note on the use of the word "broker." The terms "mortgage broker," "loan officer," and "loan originator" are used interchangeably in the business and generally mean the same thing—a person who has taken the borrower's application and originated the transaction with the subprime borrower. Brokers then arrange for a lender (like Kellner) to approve and fund the loan. A lender, however, can also act as a broker, which many of the smaller ones did, choosing to avoid the risk associated with funding a subprime loan.

Some loan officers really had the customer's best interest at heart. Others were so green they couldn't interpret a credit report or paycheck stub. Not only did we have to double- and triple-check the information provided to us, we had to help them understand the document they were submitting and whether it was acceptable to underwriting.

While Annie's account paints an accurate picture, nothing describes the sheer lunacy better than my partner Ken's trip to Houston in 2005. As you read this story, keep in mind that a loan officer in Texas must either work for a mortgage lender or have a sponsoring mortgage broker in order to operate legally. The law doesn't require the broker and loan officer to work out of the same office as long as the loan officer's license is displayed in the broker's office.

Ken describes his Houston trip this way:

I'm traveling with a new wholesale rep trying to help him get some loans from his new broker accounts. Walking into the broker's office made me realize just how screwed up this business had become.

The office is one tiny room, maybe 12 × 12. The place is a mess, unbelievably filthy and it smells of body odor. There's no place to sit down and even if I could find a spot, I'm afraid to think what I might catch. The first things I notice are the loan officer's licenses. Every square inch of his office walls is covered top to bottom, side to side, with licenses. I'm guessing there must be 250 licenses either stapled or taped to the walls.

The biggest problem was the broker's recordkeeping or lack thereof. His loan files were stacked in piles around the room and he didn't know where anything was. As we're talking, he's knocking files to the ground trying to locate deals for us to review. The place was utter chaos. I saw copies of borrowers' tax returns lying on the floor. When I asked him which file they belonged to, he didn't know.

This broker had no control over his company and it eventually cost him. The Texas Department of Savings and Mortgage Lending conducted an audit shortly after Ken's visit—no, we didn't call them, but it crossed our minds. They required him to pay some large penalties and take numerous steps to improve his operation.

Aside from not following the compliance requirements of the business, his decision to sponsor all these (mostly unqualified) loan officers was perfectly legal. The state allowed him to operate this way and he took advantage of it. The challenge for us came in supporting the loan officers since most were new and understood little about the business. Colleagues tell me he's improved his operation, but the Texas Savings & Loan web site as of December 2007 still shows him sponsoring more than 335 loan officers.

The lack of oversight became more pronounced with the proliferation of "net branch" companies, the mortgage equivalent of franchising but without the large up-front fees. These companies handled the basic business functions (accounting, IT, licensing) so that brokers were freed up to generate more business.

While some firms like Allied Home Mortgage Capital Corporation had stringent experience requirements and zero tolerance for fraudulent behavior, others provided new loan officers with easy entry to the business. Many of them allowed the loan originators to work from home. Although the practice wasn't illegal or improper, we experienced more problems working with these types of loan officers. There was a collective feeling within our company that inexperienced originators who worked from home were less competent since they seldom received proper training and support.

Rob Legg was our lead salesperson for Carteret Mortgage, a large net branch company. Here's a summary of his four-year experience calling on this customer:

> Aside from a handful of top-notch loan officers, most of their originators really struggled with the business. I had so many loan officers calling me that didn't know a tax return from a

credit report, I eventually stopped returning their messages. It amazed me that some of them could earn a paycheck.

When I left Kellner in late 2005, incidents of fraud had already hit record levels. Amazingly, it got even worse. The figures released by the MIDEX (Mortgage Industry Date Exchange) database show that mortgage fraud incident submissions were 30 percent greater in 2006 than in 2005.

Eventually more than 70 percent of all brokered loan applications submitted to us at Kellner were somehow deceptive, so everything a broker said or did needed to be double-checked and reverified. I've had several colleagues who owned subprime mortgage companies tell me this estimate is conservative compared to their own experience, especially during the last few years before the industry imploded.

I can't think of another industry where the vendor-client relationship has such a high degree of distrust. If almost three-fourths of all potential transactions are somehow fraudulent, unreliable, or misleading, it means the business model is fundamentally flawed.

While there are no statistics to support the following claim, it's highly probable that a direct correlation exists between the increased levels of fraud and the influx of new loan originators.

What Brokers Do, and What They're Supposed to Do

In theory, brokers are the best option when shopping for a mortgage loan. With access to dozens of lenders and hundreds of programs, brokers offer a one-stop alternative to applying with multiple lenders. The credit-challenged borrower has even more to gain from using a broker. The rates and fees for subprime mortgages can vary widely, and good brokers can locate the best product and price to meet the borrower's needs.

There are some disadvantages as well. Brokers have little control over the loan process, as it is the lender who must underwrite and fund the mortgage. In addition, using brokers adds one more step to the mortgage food chain, which can result in higher, not lower, costs for the borrower. Finally, since brokers are largely unregulated, it's often difficult for consumers to differentiate between the honest and the unethical loan officer until the transaction is nearly complete.

There's also a direct correlation between the type of mortgage a borrower obtains and the amount of influence a broker has over the borrower. *Conforming* or *conventional mortgages* that conform to national lending standards such as Fannie Mae's are considered plain vanilla products. Since borrowers need reasonably good credit and income to qualify, these loans are easier to transact and require less work on the part of the broker. Borrowers who present a good credit risk have options. If they feel a broker is acting inappropriately or charging excessive fees, they can easily move their loan to another mortgage company.

The subprime borrower, however, typically undergoes a different experience. The loan process can be difficult and arduous, like trying to fit a square peg into a round hole. Borrowers want a good deal, but their main concern is getting approved. Since credit scores are a major issue, most brokers will counsel their borrowers on how to act between application and closing—no major purchases, no new credit, and no credit inquiries. Any of these activities can cause the score to drop and jeopardize the loan. In addition, brokers advise their borrowers not to talk to competing brokers, since the competing broker will also pull the borrower's credit report—which can lower the borrowers credit score. This advice has merit but it also limits the subprime borrower's options. In addition, since the approval process can be a difficult and emotionally draining experience, many subprime borrowers prefer to use one loan officer to find the best deal.

The problem comes when a broker presents an offer, and the borrower has no competing offers. When there's no basis for comparison, the borrower has to trust that it's a reasonable offer. That's a lot of faith to put in a broker who has no financial liability, little regulatory oversight, and no clear fiduciary duty. When a vulnerable borrower puts a mortgage in the hands of an unscrupulous broker, the mix can be toxic.

To complicate matters, brokers became a driving force for subprime loans. By 2003, they originated only 25 percent of all prime loans but over 50 percent of all subprime mortgages. There are three reasons for this disparity. First, since conforming mortgages are a commodity, direct lenders would usually win a price war unless the broker was willing to drastically reduce his income. Second, with more than 100 wholesale subprime lenders in the market by 2003, borrowers with damaged credit had access to far more loan options through a broker than a single lender. Third, the greater income potential from subprime mortgages meant brokers had a motive to steer marginal borrowers toward this product even if they qualified for a more competitive loan with better rates and lower fees.

When salespeople in any business are left to their own devices, they'll work the system to their benefit. As the next chapter shows, this is also true of the lender's account executives. With few rules and minimal consumer protections, abusive behavior flourished. The harsh reality of brokering subprime mortgages is that many loan officers are more concerned with their own paycheck than with the best interests of the borrower.

In this chapter, I expose the world of mortgage brokers by examining their practices through the eyes of a subprime lender. You'll learn about the business of brokering mortgages, the impact of fraud on the industry, and the tactics used by brokers to secure loan approvals, which fall into three categories: honest, dysfunctional, and corrupt.

The Business of Brokering Mortgages

If there's a demand for a product or service, someone is brokering it. Whether it's real estate, technology, or sex, brokers are paid to connect people who want something with those who supply it. The service that mortgage brokers provide, however, is unique in two ways.

First, they sell a high-ticket item—mortgage debt. With a home still being the largest financial investment most people make, getting a bad deal on a loan can be an expensive mistake. Second, with over 60 percent of households owning a home, mortgage origination is a widely used service. When factored together, there is no other brokered product or service that has as large a financial impact on the majority of consumers.

By 2000, more than 250,000 mortgage brokers operated in the United States. Few states had licensing requirements, which meant the barriers to entry were minimal. Even when states started requiring licenses, the typical prerequisites were disproportionately easy to meet, such as passing a multiple-choice test and not having any felony convictions.

The income potential made brokering mortgages an attractive business. In the same way investors pay lenders a premium to buy mortgages, lenders pay brokers a yield-spread premium (YSP) to sell a higher interest rate. This applies to all mortgages, not just subprime. For example, if the market or par rate on a subprime loan is 9 percent, brokers earn 1 point in YSP by selling 9.5 percent, and 2 points for selling 10.25 percent.

So how much do brokers make per loan? It depends on how much they can charge the borrower in fees and the interest rate they can sell. The competitive nature of conforming mortgages usually limits brokers to making no more than 2 points. In a slower market, most of them struggle to make between 1 and 1.5 points. Since subprime borrowers are primarily concerned about getting approved, they aren't as rate sensitive as prime borrowers, enabling brokers to charge them higher rates and fees.

Despite the disclosures the industry has created, there is still much confusion. Until a final settlement statement (the HUD-1) is ready for review, borrowers don't know how much the broker will make on the loan. While consumers should receive a Good Faith Estimate (GFE) of costs within three days of application, each state treats the disclosure of YSP differently. In Texas and some other states, brokers are allowed to indicate they'll make a range between "0 to 3%," which is nonsensical. Why have a disclosure when it doesn't tell the consumer anything?

To make matters worse, the broker is not obligated to honor the rates and fees on the disclosure. Of course, this applies to the lender as well, but abuse is more common at the broker level. As long as the borrower signs a corrected GFE that corresponds with the final HUD-1, a broker can change the deal at any time. For borrowers who are more vulnerable, the system has few protections.

How Brokers Operate

Once the borrower's application is taken and a credit report has been ordered, most loans follow a similar path. There is no standard process, but unless the deal is identified early on as a government loan—either through the Federal Housing Authority (FHA) or Veterans Administration (VA)—brokers usually follow these steps:

- The loan is run through Desktop Underwriter, Fannie Mae's automated underwriting (AU) system, or through Loan Prospector, Freddie Mac's AU system. An approval through either program classifies the loan as a conforming or conventional mortgage, which means the deal meets the guidelines established by these agencies.

- If neither system provides an approval, the broker can still seek FHA approval if he's approved by the Department of Housing and Urban Development (HUD) and the loan meets the requirements. Before subprime became popular, FHA was the best alternative for credit-challenged borrowers.

- The broker can send the loan to a subprime or Alt-A lender or use the lender's AU system to approve the loan. Lenders like Countrywide and RFC developed proprietary systems to underwrite their nonagency loans.

When we opened in 2000, AU systems were almost nonexistent for subprime mortgages. To get a loan prequalified, brokers relied on the lender's account executive to review the borrower's application and credit report. Handling difficult transactions through a manual process meant underwriting was a hit or miss experience. There are no official statistics, but it's widely believed the loan fallout rate (the percentage of brokered loans submitted to subprime lenders for underwriting that did not fund) averaged 50 percent.

The high fallout rate meant subprime became synonymous with poor service. With many account executives lacking the expertise to handle complex transactions, brokers searched for reps who understood the business. The inefficiencies led some brokers to send loans through multiple lenders at the same time. This "throw it against the wall and see if it sticks" mentality also contributed to the high fallout rate.

Over the next five years, technology would become an integral part of the business. By 2005, most subprime lenders had developed their own proprietary AU systems. Even smaller companies like mine who couldn't afford to build their own systems found alternative solutions. RFC allowed us to customize the look of their AU system, Assetwise, to match our branding campaign. When brokers used the system on our web site, it looked like we spent millions developing the technology.

While many brokers welcomed the use of technology for underwriting subprime loans, the systems took a while to catch on since every lender had its own version (which required training) and brokers used multiple lenders. For conforming loans, brokers had little choice—there were only two AU systems and loans had to be approved through one of them. Since AU systems were new to subprime, few lenders made their use mandatory when they first came out. Even when they did, brokers relied on their reps to help get loans approved.

The independent nature of brokers meant loyalty was a scarce commodity. With over 100 subprime lenders to choose from, most brokers would try a new company if they could make more money. As a result, the competition for broker business became fierce. One of my clients used to joke that he spent so much time fielding sales calls from reps, he didn't have time to solicit his own customers. In large markets like Dallas, a broker could easily see a dozen different reps every day.

The best brokers, however, operated with a different philosophy. They worked hard to develop relationships with referral sources such as realtors. To maintain the business, they had to consistently produce results. To do this required having a few subprime lenders who could deliver on what they promised. The high fallout rate that lenders experienced for subprime loans was driven by the difficult nature of the deals, but also by ineffective account executives. As the industry grew, the subprime business attracted its fair share of useless salespeople. The worst scenario for any broker was not closing a Realtor's purchase transaction because they trusted an incompetent rep. The smart brokers avoided putting their business relationships in jeopardy by only working with a handful of top-notch account executives.

Mortgage Fraud

It's easy to understand why the lending industry attracts unethical behavior—hundreds of millions of dollars in business are transacted on a daily basis. There are no official estimates, but it's widely believed that lenders lose tens of millions of dollars annually as a result of fraudulent activity.

For our purposes, mortgage fraud is any activity that's intended to deceive or mislead a mortgage lender. When stories about mortgage fraud make the news, they usually portray the more heinous examples. These scams often involve multiple parties—brokers, appraisers, and title companies. Even though a thorough quality control (QC) review increases the likelihood a fraudulent loan will be identified prior to closing, it's impossible to catch every one. At some point, most subprime lenders were victimized by one of these scams.

While this type of fraud could prove costly, it was only a small piece of a bigger problem. The subtler forms of fraud, more difficult to detect, could also create problems for lenders. The following are just a few examples:

- A borrower indicating that he will occupy a property when he's purchasing it as an investment.
- Falsifying a borrower's employment history by having a friend or relative who owns a business say the person works there.
- Hiding a critical piece of information or not disclosing something about the loan and hoping the lender won't find out.

The last one gave lenders fits. If a broker is hiding something from the lender, how do they know what to look for? Performing a thorough QC review can help but isn't always effective. At times the lender-broker relationship resembles a game of hide-and-go-seek. When brokers try to conceal critical information, lenders search for clues to piece together the story.

Here is an example of how this works. A broker submitted a loan to us indicating the borrower was doing a cash-out refinance on his primary residence. The borrower also owned another property, which he had purchased three years earlier. At the time he purchased this property his credit was damaged so the seller agreed to carry the note. The borrower turned the second property into a rental when he purchased his current residence. Unfortunately, the person who rented the home moved out unexpectedly, leaving him in a jam. With no tenant to replace the lost income, the borrower fell two months behind on the mortgage for the rental property.

While filling out the loan application, the borrower disclosed the late payments to the broker. Since the mortgage was privately held, there was no record of it on the borrower's credit report. The broker asked his customer, "What's the chance the note holder will fill out the VOM (verification of mortgage) and say you've paid on time?" He rationalized to the borrower that since he was getting cash to catch up with the mortgage payments, the note holder would be motivated to help. Somehow fraud always seemed easier to justify when someone else had to do it. When the broker discovered the note holder was (surprise!) a man of principle and wouldn't commit fraud, he devised an alternate plan. He submitted the loan application and left the schedule of real estate section blank. With no record of the mortgage on his credit report, we didn't know the rental property existed. The broker was committing fraud through omission, and by signing the loan application, so was the borrower.

The broker thought he fooled everyone. What he didn't consider was the due diligence our underwriter would conduct on the loan. Part of her standard procedure was to use the county web site to obtain the property's tax-assessed value. When she searched using the borrower's name, both properties showed up, which caused the loan to be denied.

The broker swore he did nothing wrong, insisting the borrower never disclosed the rental information. In a phone conversation with the borrower, he explained to me in great detail exactly what happened. It was obvious the broker had concocted the plan. Having previously suspected him of questionable activity, we terminated his account.

We were lucky. The underwriter could have searched by the subject property address, in which case the rental would have remained a mystery. Had the property been located in a different county, it also would have gone undetected. With no system for sharing this information with other lenders, the broker could easily take the loan file to another company, which he did. A month later, our rep confirmed through a third party source that the loan closed with New Century.

Broker Tactics

The tactics brokers used for subprime loans can be divided into three categories: honest, dysfunctional, or corrupt. If a broker was dysfunctional, it doesn't mean they acted improperly on every loan file—a broker could be honest on one deal and dysfunctional on the next. The tactics a broker used depended on two factors: what was required to close the loan, and how far the broker was willing to go. Of course, since brokers could operate with few consequences from their actions, subprime lenders treated them with a high degree of suspicion.

Honest Brokers

About 30 percent of all subprime loan applications require no manipulation or deception on the part of the broker because the borrower meets the credit requirements, documentation is readily obtainable, and the property values are easily justified. While few deals in subprime are a slam-dunk, these loans were usually the easiest to complete.

Some brokers consistently operate with a high degree of professionalism. They understand the importance of treating the customer right. When the borrower chooses a loan program, it's an informed decision. The fees these brokers charge are reasonable for the service they provide. Ask customers to rate their service experience and these brokers get high marks across the board.

As a lender, working with this type of broker means getting the entire story the first time. If there's a problem with the deal, the broker brings it up right away. These honest brokers treat the borrower and the lender as if they have a fiduciary duty to both parties. Full disclosure from start to finish is the only way these brokers conduct business.

This could describe a strong salesperson in any industry, not just mortgage finance. Treating a customer fairly, communicating honestly with vendors, and doing the right thing for everyone are how things should work. Unfortunately, these brokers are in the minority.

The goal of any lender is to work with brokers who consistently deliver credible deals. Even if the loan officer didn't produce a lot of business, just knowing he would keep the lender out of harm's way was invaluable. One of my customers, Ryan Miller, a former branch manager for Allied Home Mortgage Capital in Florence, South Carolina, epitomized the honest broker. One event early in our relationship convinced me he was a cut above the rest.

We had just closed the Jenna Matthews loan and were preparing to release the funds when Ryan called me. He had just gotten a phone call from the closer at the attorney's office because she overheard a conversation between the borrower and another employee in the office. Ms. Matthews was so excited about her good news that she had to tell someone—the day before closing she found a person to rent the property she was buying. The problem was that she had signed an occupancy affidavit indicating she intended to live in the property.

Before calling me, Ryan contacted the borrower, confronted her with the facts, and confirmed the story. We had no choice but to deny the loan. So why did the borrower lie? By leading us to believe she would live in the property, Ms. Matthews could buy the home with no money down and get a lower interest rate. Had the deal closed, it's likely our investor would have made us repurchase the loan.

Ryan performed the ultimate selfless act. Since the loan didn't close, he made no money. He was scheduled to close only two loans that month, which meant his income would be cut in half. He could have ignored the situation or delayed calling me and no one would have known the difference. Instead, he chose to do the right thing.

By proving he was an honest broker, Ryan endeared himself to us. Over the next five years, he received a level of service that made up for the lost revenue. Whether it meant the underwriting department did a rush approval or an employee came in early to prepare closing documents, his good deed served him well in the long run. He wasn't our biggest customer but that didn't matter. We knew he had our backs, and in this business, that is worth its weight in gold.

Dysfunctional Brokers

With subprime mortgages, the majority of brokers operated in a dysfunctional manner. Since this can describe a broad range of impropriety, I'll define a dysfunctional act as anything that creates an additional layer of risk for the lender or does not serve the best interest of the borrower.

Even the most ethical brokers can be tempted to push in one area or cut corners in another. The practice of massaging loans, making them appear different from what they are, becomes standard operating procedure. With little accountability for their actions, brokers are left to decide how far they're willing to go.

There are three types of dysfunctional brokers: pushers, withholders, and manipulators. They aren't mutually exclusive—a broker could act as a pusher and manipulator at the same time. Brokers used these dysfunctional tactics in approximately 65 percent of all loans sent to subprime lenders. What follows are examples of each.

Pushers

The word pusher has several connotations. It can represent any good salesperson who keeps selling the lender on the merits of a loan. The pusher will work the deal from every angle until the lender either approves or denies it. The act of pushing a lender isn't dysfunctional—it's the broker's job.

A loan can also be pushed when a broker's actions increase the risk to the lender. Some brokers develop a reputation for pushing. After closing a few loans for this type of broker, a pattern would emerge—every deal submitted either stretched the guidelines to the limit or required a loan exception. When our staff discussed these brokers, they'd frequently refer to them in conversation by saying, "I know who you're talking about. He's the guy whose loans are always pushed."

Compared to other dysfunctional types of brokers, the pusher was the least harmful. In most cases, the lender had all the correct information to make a lending decision. The lender's risk increased when the pusher also withheld or manipulated information in order to get a loan approved.

Our Best Customer

Steve McKay was our best customer. In the six years we were in business, he closed more loans with us than any other broker. Our second-best customer produced just over half as many loans. Steve was a pusher extraordinaire.

We knew what to expect from Steve because he had done business with my partner Ken for 10 years. Experience told us we could trust him about 90 percent of the time. While Steve was not inclined to put us in harm's way, he wasn't motivated to keep us out of it either. Other lenders weren't always so lucky.

In 2002, Steve needed additional office space to accommodate his growing staff. He bought a single-family residence, informing the lender he intended to occupy it as his primary residence. As mentioned earlier, any borrower who intends to live in a property must sign an occupancy affidavit at closing. After closing on the purchase, Steve hired a contractor who converted the home into offices for his employees. He had never intended to live in the property. We discovered this only because Steve chose to tell Ken, which is an odd situation—a broker told his best lender how he defrauded another mortgage company so he could get a better deal. Even if we had the nerve to commit fraud, I can't imagine bragging about it to our top investor.

Here is Ken's account of working with Steve:

> Steve is a career mortgage broker. He was very methodical in how he pushed lenders to get things done. If he had a loan with multiple issues, he'd figure out the best way to sell us on the deal. He knew how to spin deals to make them sound better than they really were.
>
> The one area he consistently pushed was appraisals. An incompetent broker would submit appraisals that were so overvalued most lenders wouldn't believe them. Steve was too smart for that. Since property valuation is not an exact science, he knew every lender had a certain variance they would accept. His appraised values came in high enough to make the deal work, but not so high that a lender or investor wouldn't accept it.

While Steve knew exactly how and where he could push, he also understood how far he could go before he crossed the line. That's what made him an effective pusher.

Here are some other tactics that brokers used to push loans:

- A couple wanted to pull equity out of their property to pay some bills, but were concerned about the size of the loan payment. The broker convinced them to take an adjustable rate mortgage that came with a lower start rate, allowing them to get more cash. Since the broker's commission was based on the loan amount, selling the higher loan amount made him more money.

- A borrower purchased a home and two days before closing the lender received the appraisal and the property appeared to be overvalued. The lender ordered a field review through a third party service to confirm the value, which would take five days to complete. Since the property seller was scheduled to purchase a home on the same day using the proceeds from his sale, the broker tried to convince the lender that the deal had to close on time or it would create a domino effect, causing all of the transactions to fall apart. If the broker believed the property was significantly overvalued, he knew an independent appraisal review would likely reveal it, thus jeopardizing the deal and his income. Pushing the lender to close the deal was his way of insuring a paycheck.

The challenge was determining whether or not the deal would fall apart if the closing was delayed. Getting this answer usually required the lender to initially deny the broker's request in order to learn how real the threat was. The lender either closed the loan as scheduled and hoped the field review substantiated the appraised value, or let the deal collapse and risked aggravating the broker, borrower, and Realtor. In most cases, buyers and sellers had so much invested in the transaction, both financially and emotionally, they were willing to wait a few extra days.

Withholders

If a broker withholds information, the lender does not have the data he needs to make an underwriting decision. This creates a conundrum. What should a lender look for when he doesn't know what's missing? Without all the facts needed to make an informed decision, lenders are put at greater risk.

Gathering income, employment, and credit documentation will usually tell the lender most of the story, but there are still opportunities for nondisclosure. If a broker is privy to information and thinks the lender will deny the loan if he discloses it, what should he do? Tell the lender and run the risk of a denial or pretend it doesn't exist? If it's the difference between getting paid or not getting paid, brokers are likely to stay quiet.

For some brokers, withholding information is easier to justify than blatantly committing fraud. Most acts of deception require the broker to do something, like alter a pay stub or manipulate a verification of employment (VOE). Nondisclosure only requires silence. The following loan scenario shows how a broker's decision to keep quiet proved to be costly.

The Robinsons wanted to refinance their home to get some cash. The broker put Mr. Robinson in a stated income program since he was self-employed and couldn't prove his income through his tax returns. Mrs. Robinson's credit was poor, so she was removed from the loan application altogether. When the loan closed the couple received $25,000.

The Robinsons never made a mortgage payment. After doing some research, we found out what happened. At the time of loan application, the couple was planning to divorce. Their plan was that she'd retain the home, he'd keep the money from the refinance, and she'd be responsible for the mortgage. The problem was she couldn't afford the payment based on her income. In separate conversations with the Robinsons, they each confirmed that the broker was briefed on their plan.

When we confronted the broker, he admitted knowing there was a problem, but thought they were trying to work things out. By pleading ignorance the broker absolved himself of any wrongdoing. Since there was no legal separation agreement, it was his word against theirs. The broker knew exactly what he was doing. Disclosing their plan would have jeopardized the deal, so he said nothing. Had we known the facts, the loan would have been declined because Mrs. Robinson wasn't able to qualify on her own. By the time the foreclosure was complete and the property resold, we had lost $75,000. That's a heavy price to pay for nondisclosure.

Brokers can withhold information from lenders in a number of ways such as these:

- The broker encourages a borrower to obtain a separate loan to cover the down payment for a home purchase. By not disclosing the separate loan on the mortgage application and timing the loan to close shortly before the mortgage, the broker prevents the lender from learning about the additional debt.

- The broker reviews borrowers' income documents and determines they don't make enough money to qualify, so he puts them into a stated income loan and never sends the income documents to the lender. While stated income loans are a standard industry offering, this scenario assumes the broker has confirmed the borrower cannot afford the payment.

Manipulators

Loan manipulation means either information is altered to make the lender believe the loan is less risky or the broker's actions are deceptive and potentially damaging to the consumer. A broker willing to do this takes fraud to the next level. Such a broker is motivated purely by income with no regard for the lender or the consumer. Unlike the first two categories of dysfunctional brokers, manipulation requires the broker to willfully exploit a situation.

Manipulation comes in many forms. Here are a few of the most common types:

- Falsifying or altering income documentation. Desktop publishing programs allow for near-perfect replication of pay stubs and W-2s.
- Placing an unsuspecting borrower into an adjustable rate mortgage without explaining how it works.
- Pulling a bait and switch by disclosing a lower rate and fee structure to a borrower and then increasing the figures shortly before closing.

The last example is painful to witness. Since the broker has the relationship with the borrower, lenders aren't expected to have any direct contact with this person prior to closing. If the lender needs something from the borrower, the broker serves as intermediary. This helps preserve the broker-borrower relationship and prevents the lender from poaching the broker's customer.

When brokers pull a bait and switch, lenders have few options. They could go around the broker, but that is a dangerous tactic. Once a lender is known for doing end runs, they risk alienating other brokers. The only other option would be to inactivate the broker. This also poses a dilemma, since unless the lender waited until the loan closed, he would penalize the consumer by not completing the deal.

After 14 years in the mortgage business, I'm convinced the process of buying a first home can be one of the most stressful situations consumers experience. After going through all the steps to find a home and get approved, imagine the distress borrowers feel when they discover the loan terms have changed at the last minute. What options do they have? A borrower with damaged credit who had struggled to get approved feels trapped. Between the earnest money that has been put down, the landlord who's been given notice, and the moving company storing their worldly possessions, they have committed themselves to the process. Threatening to report the broker to the attorney general unless the original deal is honored is usually all that's needed, but many borrowers don't know that this is an option. Since the broker isn't required to meet the figures disclosed on the Good Faith Estimate, borrowers with damaged credit become easy targets.

The manipulators were a concern to lenders for several reasons. First, they could inflict enormous damage. Anyone willing to throw a lender or consumer under the bus is a serious threat. Second, just because a broker manipulated loans didn't mean he did it on every deal. Some brokers were chameleons, changing colors when it suited them best, and any lenders that let their guard down could easily be victimized.

Jeff McDaniel was just this kind of broker. After a year of doing business together, we started developing some trust. He represented himself as a highly ethical person and never gave us any reason to doubt him. But when he called one afternoon and said, "I've got a loan ready to close," it meant another lender had just declined the deal. A loan can only close if a broker has a complete file, which means it was originally sent to another mortgage company. Just because a lender denied the loan didn't mean it was fraudulent, but it did mean we had to dig deep to find out why the lender wouldn't take it.

Jeff mentioned the loan was turned down for credit reasons but we suspected something else. The borrower had only fair credit, but it should have been good enough for any subprime lender. Something didn't smell right about this deal. It was possible that the borrower, a single woman, was buying a 6,000-square-foot home, but not likely. The appraiser called it a single-family residence, but the picture of the front of the property was taken from so far away it was hard to make out any details. Since the interior photos were also taken from odd angles, we suspected the appraiser was hiding something.

By coincidence, Ken's wife was visiting a friend in the city where the property was located, so we had her take a look. She drove by the house and discovered it wasn't a residence but a small office building. At some point it had been a single-family residence, but it had been converted to individual suites with living quarters in the rear. Each company that rented space had a separate entrance at the front of the property. This explained why the appraiser took the picture from so far away—he didn't want the lender to see the company nameplates on the doors.

There is no doubt the appraisal was manipulated. Residential appraisers would never do this type of work unless they were completely incompetent or influenced by someone. Since Jeff ordered the appraisal, he's the only person who could have planned this fraud.

When a broker is caught red-handed, the follow-up calls are usually memorable. Watching brokers attempt to lie their way out of a situation makes for an interesting study in human behavior. In this case, Jeff didn't know that Ken's wife had seen the property, so we tried to trap him, hoping for a confession. Even though he was backed into a corner and fumbled his way through the call, he tried to turn it around by blaming the borrower. He wanted us to believe that she conspired with the appraiser, but his argument made no sense. Brokers drive this process and it was clear who was running the scam.

Jeff is the worst kind of manipulator. He spent a year gaining our confidence, making us believe he was trustworthy. Faced with a chance to make a $15,000 commission check, he finally showed us his true colors.

Whether it was the borrowers, brokers, or a combination of the two that contributed to the trend toward manipulation, it's easy to understand why this business could turn anyone into a cynic.

Corrupt Brokers

While any broker who manipulates a file can be classified as corrupt, I reserve this category for the worst offenders. There is also one significant difference between a manipulative broker and a corrupt one. A manipulative broker will determine what actions need to be taken for a lender to approve a loan. Even though the deal is fraudulent, the borrower has the intention of making payments. The corrupt broker is crafting a plan to generate income by inflicting financial harm on a lender. It's unlikely a payment will ever be made. Fortunately, the tactics these brokers used accounted for only about 5 percent of all subprime loans.

These brokers have no redeeming qualities—they're immoral and malicious. The best way to illustrate their actions is to list some of the losses they caused our company.

- Tim Booker purchased a home in south Dallas. The only problem was that Mr. Booker was deployed on a naval ship in the Middle East when his closing documents were signed. His uncle, the mortgage broker who originated the loan, used him as a straw buyer, which meant he never intended to occupy or make payments on the property. He arranged to have someone else sign all the closing documents. Cost to Kellner Mortgage Investments: $13,000.

- In 2001, we wrote a mortgage for Thomas Arnold, also a straw buyer. This loan was completely fabricated. The appraisal we received was for a completely different property. His income documentation and bank statements had been altered. The broker, buyer, appraiser, and realtor all conspired to perpetrate this fraud. The loan closed six months after we opened, when our QC procedures were lax. It was a very expensive lesson. Cost to Kellner Mortgage Investments: $100,000.

• In 2003, our company sold a property we owned in a deal put together by Kurt Davis, a local broker. The couple that bought the house claimed they never signed the loan documents and that someone forged their signatures. We suspected Mr. Davis was the guilty party, but he died shortly before the trial started. When he structured the deal, it required us to carry a second mortgage. When Washington Mutual foreclosed on the property, we lost our lien. Cost to Kellner Mortgage Investments: $90,000.

These brokers didn't care about the wreckage left in their wake. They would use whatever tactics were necessary to plan their schemes. While some were linked to organized crime, many were small operations that moved from lender to lender, looking for their next target.

Since these brokers were in the business of fabricating deals, most of them kept their distance from lenders. On one occasion, however, I did have a chance to interact with one of these operations. Having just opened our company, I connected with one of the largest mortgage brokers in Cleveland, Ohio, a branch office for Country Home Mortgage. After building a relationship with Luther, a person who portrayed himself as the branch manager, I flew to Cleveland hoping to further the relationship. The trip still ranks as the strangest and most bizarre event during my mortgage career.

What Did I Get Myself Into?

Stepping off the plane in the Cleveland, I'm greeted by Jeff, who introduces himself as the VP of Sales. Since he doesn't look old enough to drink, I'm surprised a guy so young is running the sales team.

On the drive to the office, I find out this is his first job in the mortgage business. He tells me, "This is actually my first job in sales. Before that I worked in my uncle's service station." Yesterday he's pumping gas and today he's running a sales team. Maybe he's a quick learner. Who am I to judge?

We get to the office and join everyone for lunch at the restaurant next door. Being 6′4″ and 230 pounds, I'm rarely intimidated by someone else's size, but this is one of those moments. As Luther stands up to greet me, he's my height but at least 40 to 50 pounds heavier. With his big bushy beard and flannel shirt, I can't help but think he looks like Grizzly Adams on steroids.

I take the seat across from their title rep, Suzanne. After a few minutes of conversation, I can't help but notice her wedding ring since it's the largest single diamond I've ever seen. Being a curious guy, I ask her, "So, Suzanne what does your husband do for a living?" As though it were staged, all five people within earshot of our conversation burst into laughter. Suzanne says, "Really sweetheart, it's healthier for you to not ask that question." Hold the mortgage train a minute. Did she just say healthier? When it becomes clear she isn't kidding, my head starts to fill with images of cement-filled shoes and me sinking to the bottom of the Cuyahoga. Maybe changing the subject is a good idea.

After we leave the restaurant and go back into his building, Luther leads me toward his office in the back of the suite. As we approach the last office, I'm struck by the enormous size of his door. This massive steel contraption looks like it belongs on the front of a vault, not in an office. Luther sees me eyeing it and says, "Oh, you like the door? I got it out of an old bank that closed down. The great thing about this is, short of a rocket launcher, nobody's getting in."

Rocket launcher? Why does a mortgage broker need a door that could protect Fort Knox? Sure, we're in the money business, but it's not like we print the stuff or keep any lying around. Looking around inside the office, I don't see anything of value outside of a bizarre collection of knives hanging on the wall.

"Cool knife collection, Luther. Where did you pick these up?" I ask.

"Oh you like them? This one's my favorite. I like to use it for target practice."

I turn around in time to see him pull this knife out of its wall mount and hurl it toward the corner of his office. With a loud thud, it smacks into the middle of a wooden board.

"Holy shit!" I yell.

Luther practically pees his pants he's laughing so loud. Once he calms down he says, "Sorry about that, Rich, I just couldn't help myself."After my heart starts beating again, it occurs to me he's probably done the knife routine before.

Watching the office in operation, it seems to me the ads they run must be paying off. Calls are steadily coming in, which means the loan officers keep busy. They bring me deals to qualify, but I'm surprised how little they know about the business. Then again, considering the head of sales is 20 years old and is still learning how to spell mortgage, why should I be surprised? This is not an impressive team.

That evening at dinner, Luther decides to drop another bombshell. "You seem like a good guy and you'll eventually find this out, so it's best you hear it from me," he says. "About eight years ago, a former business partner set me up and I did a few years in the federal pen."

He talks about how he almost killed the meanest guy in the joint, came to terms with his own mortality, and now lives every day to the fullest. None of it's really getting through—I'm still stuck on the part about going to jail. As a relatively conservative Ivy League grad, having come up through the ranks of GE and GM, I'm used to conducting business a certain way. This never included having knives thrown by convicted felons or working behind impenetrable steel doors. Somehow the world of Jack Welch and Six Sigma seemed a long way off.

After dinner we go back to his office to retrieve a file and no sooner do we arrive than his cell phone rings.

"This is Luther. Wait a minute, Gena, calm down. Tell me what happened? When? All right, I'll take care of it." He hangs up and starts dialing a number.

As though magically transformed into a different person, this bear of a man begins talking in a very subdued and gentle tone. "Oh, good evening, ma'am. I'm so sorry to call this late. Oh yes, it's Luther. Is His Honor still awake?"

His Honor? Is he calling a judge at home at 10:30 in the evening?

When the judge picks up the phone Luther starts talking. "Good evening, Your Honor. Yes, sorry to disturb you." He spends the next minute telling the judge how some friends of his had a misunderstanding. The husband found himself in jail after a typical domestic dispute. The wife called the police and now realizes it was all a big mistake. There is a long silence as Luther listens intently to the judge. He finishes by saying, "Thank you for your help, sir. You have a good evening as well."

Luther turns off his phone and says to me, "Well it's a good thing he was still up or that schmuck would've spent the whole night in the can. He'll be out in the next hour or two."

Forget about the pubescent VP of sales, the knife throwing, the jail stint, the impenetrable steel door, the enormous diamond for the title rep married to God only knows who, this is now the highlight of my day. I've just witnessed a convicted felon call a judge to help get a buddy out of jail, apparently with success. My dossier has a total of two speeding tickets. It's clear that I'm way out of my league. Finding out about all of this in less than 12 hours makes me wonder what else there is to know about this guy. My gut tells me to drop him like a bad habit but, having just opened our company, I'm desperate for business.

The next morning I fly back to Dallas. Within two weeks we catch Luther trying to pass off a doctored bank statement. Like every other broker who committed fraud and got caught, he tries to convince us it's not his fault. This time it's the loan processor who did it. After dealing with hundreds of dysfunctional and corrupt brokers, just once I'd like to meet one who said, "Yes, that's right, I was the guy who did it." Recently, after not having spoken to Luther since late 2000, I Googled his name to see what I could find out. An article published in the News-Herald in Ohio related that he had been serving 17 months in prison for theft when he was caught on tape trying to hire a hit man to kill the judge who sentenced him. I still wonder if that was the same judge he talked to on the phone that night. He accepted a deal in this case, according to the News-Herald, pleading guilty to four counts of intimidation and one count of retaliation. He also pleaded guilty to charges in an unrelated real estate fraud case where he was accused of racketeering. Through the plea agreements, he was able to get the DA to drop over 200 additional charges against him ranging from conspiracy to attempted felonious assault on a police officer.

Apparently, Luther had been keeping himself very busy.

Losing Faith in Humanity

When I initially wrote this chapter, two customers stood out as examples of honest brokers. In addition to Ryan Miller, whom you read about earlier, Richard Bell was my second choice.

As an award-winning branch manager for Allied Home Mortgage Capital in the Houston area, Richard was more than a customer. He was someone I aspired to be like—a truly successful entrepreneur with a work ethic unlike anyone's I had ever known. I'm a Type A personality, but nothing compared to him.

In the four years I funded his loans, we went far beyond the typical lender-broker relationship. He was a close personal friend. While Richard did his residential subprime loans through my company, he made his big money in commercial development. From hospitals to restaurants, he became a mover and shaker in the Houston area. There were numerous articles in various Houston-area publications depicting him as a pillar in the community. One businesswoman went so far as to say that Houston is lucky to have him.

In November 2004, my wife and I spent a weekend with him and his wife, Joni, on their 65-foot yacht. At the time, it ranked as one of the most memorable trips in our 14 years of marriage. Cruising between Houston and Galveston on the biggest boat in the entire marina was enough to make anyone desire to have what he had achieved. When I sold my interest in Kellner in late 2005, I narrowed my future employment options to three opportunities. One of them included moving my family to Houston and going into business with Richard. We seriously considered the opportunity but chose something else instead.

In our four years of working together, I never suspected Richard of anything questionable. In one instance, he called me on a loan in process and said he needed to cancel the file. He had just caught the borrower trying to pass off phony pay stubs and did not want me to get stuck with a fraudulent deal. At the time, I didn't have the pay stubs in my possession so it was easy to conclude that he had covered my backside.

Not having spoken with Richard in more than a year, I tried to locate him in early 2008. Since all of his phone numbers had been disconnected, I turned again to Google to see what I could find out.

When I learned that he had pleaded guilty a few weeks earlier to one count of bank fraud and one count of engaging in monetary transactions in property derived from specific unlawful activity, I was stunned. When his 32-page federal indictment was unsealed and I was able to read it, I couldn't believe the fraud he was accused of perpetrating.

Seeing this news prompted me to dig deeper. After reading numerous postings from residents on a local Houston-area blog, I discovered a whole other side to Richard. I now understand why some people are called con artists. Like any professional who practices his craft in seek of perfection, Richard's path of destruction left a wide and devastating trail. The stories that surfaced, from accusations of horrendous spousal abuse to a myriad of investors and neighbors that had been duped, made his life sound like something out of a Grisham novel.

Why would anyone with his level of intelligence falsify most of the information on his loan application? The indictment covered everything from his pay stubs and tax returns to cashiers checks that had been scanned and subsequently forged. He originally worked in a banking environment, in "Compliance" no less. He knew that banks have extensive audit requirements and would eventually connect the dots.

Richard was originally charged with more than six counts of bank fraud but struck a deal to reduce everything down to two charges. When sentencing comes in June 2008, he could face up to 35 years in jail.

I was lucky to have avoided the carnage of Richard Bell. As with other brokers before him, I could easily have been thrown under the proverbial fraud-mobile, but was somehow spared. I have witnessed more than most when it comes to the greed this industry has to offer, and after a while nothing seems to surprise me. But after reading about Richard, it is hard not to lose some faith in humanity.

Making Chicken Salad Out of Chicken Shit: The Art of Creative Financing

The subprime lending industry has received volumes of press coverage. From the brokers who wrote the loans to the investors who securitized them, every level of the food chain has been scrutinized. However, there's one critical component that's been largely overlooked—how borrowers who initially didn't qualify for mortgages became eligible for financing. While stories of consumers who took stated income loans are well documented, the strategies used to qualify borrowers were much more complex. This chapter explores these methods and shows how difficult loans were massaged to make them saleable on the secondary market.

By 2000, the industry had become matrix driven, which meant lenders took a borrower's credit profile (credit score, bankruptcies, foreclosures, and so on) and put it on a grid to determine his credit grade. The higher the grade, the smaller the down payment (or equity) required and the better the interest rate. What happened when borrowers didn't have enough money for a down payment because they were graded too low? Assuming there was no rich uncle to help out, the choices were clear: deny the loan, commit fraud, or get creative.

If there is an art to the business of subprime lending, it's making something out of nothing. While I worked for RFC on the investor side of the business, we focused on buying closed loan files that met our guidelines. By the time the underwriters saw the deals, they'd already been massaged, squeezed, pushed, pulled, and manicured into a presentable state. Until I worked directly with brokers, I had no idea what creative financing entailed. My sales manager Rob Legg referred to the process as "making chicken salad out of chicken shit." It lacks poetry but epitomizes the true nature of the business.

This first section of this chapter explains the basic principles of risk management and how they apply to subprime mortgages. The next section reviews multiple case studies and shows the different techniques used to make difficult loans work. The final section examines residential appraisals and the methods used to manipulate a property's value.

These strategies were implemented by mortgage brokers, lender's account executives, underwriters, loans processors, and appraisers. The process of massaging loans to qualify borrowers became standard practice in the subprime industry. It was an integral part of making tough deals work.

Understanding Risk

Everything in mortgage lending revolves around the four Cs—collateral, capacity, character, and credit. Collateral is the property used as security against the loan. Capacity is a borrower's ability to pay the mortgage, determined by his income. Character is whether the lender believes a borrower is likely to repay the loan based on past performance. Credit is a borrower's payment history reflected by credit scores and overall credit profile. These fundamental principles are collectively used to determine a lender's underwriting decision.

While all four Cs are important, collateral tops the list. Since subprime borrowers typically face multiple challenges, accurately determining a property's value is vital to the process. In many cases, property value is one of the few redeeming qualities in a subprime loan.

Every subprime loan starts with analyzing credit. It's comprised of the following components: credit score; mortgage (or rental) history; previous bankruptcies and foreclosures; plus collections, charge-offs, and judgments. While every investor has his own specific guidelines for assessing risk, each of these components factors into their thinking. Some put greater emphasis on certain areas, but they all share the same basic philosophy. As a borrower goes from performing well (good score, no bankruptcies) to having problems in one or more areas, the risk goes up, which causes them to get a lower credit grade.

Figure 4.1 is a credit matrix my company used for RFC's subprime product line in 2005, but it's been simplified for easier reading. To qualify for a credit grade, a borrower needed to meet the minimum requirements in each category. For example, to be an A+ borrower you had to have a minimum 600 credit score, no late mortgage or rental payments in the last 12 months, no bankruptcies or foreclosures in the last three years, and all adverse credit (collections or charge-offs) over $500 in the last 24 months should be paid off prior to closing the loan. If a borrower had twice been 30 days late on a mortgage during the last year but met all other requirements, he received an A– grade.

The last row is labeled maximum loan-to-value (LTV). Expressed as a percentage, LTV is calculated by dividing the loan amount by the property's purchase price or appraised value, whichever is lower. The actual matrix is much more complex as

	Purchase, Rate/Term, and Equity Refinance						
Credit Grade	A+	A	A–	B	B–	C	C–
Credit Score	600	600	580	560	560	540	520
12 Months Housing History	0 × 30	1 × 30 non-rolling	2 × 30 rolling	30s allowed	1 × 60	60s allowed	1 × 90 non-rolling
BK-7 Disc.	>3 Years	>1 Year	>1 Year	>1 Year	>1 Year	>1 Year	>1 Year
BK-13 File	>3 Years	>1 Year	>1 Year	>1 Year	>1 Year	>1 Year	Must be paid
Foreclosure		>3 Years	>3 Years	>2 Years	>2 Years	>2 Years	>1 Year
Adverse Credit 24 Months	Pay at closing if > $500	Pay at closing if > $1,000	Pay at closing if > $1,500	Pay at closing if > $2,500	Pay at closing if > $2,500	Pay at closing if > $5,000	Pay at closing if > $10,000
Maximum Loan to Value	100%	100%	95%	90%	85%	80%	70%

Figure 4.1   Credit Matrix

LTVs are broken down further based on loan amount, property type, and income documentation.

As borrowers moved down the grading scale (A+ to C–), the mortgage became a riskier proposition. To compensate, lenders required a larger down payment (or more equity if it was a refinance) and a higher interest rate. On the flip side, borrowers wanted to move up the grading scale to get better terms. Massaging a loan file means artificially improving the areas that contribute to the lower credit grade (low score, excessive collections). That's how you make chicken salad.

There's one final factor to consider and that's depth of credit. Investors required borrowers to have a minimum number of acceptable trade lines. A trade line is an installment loan (such as a car payment) or a revolving account (such as a credit card). The number of required trade lines varied between investors, but usually ranged from three to five.

The policy made sense on several levels. First, a history of paying multiple creditors helps validate the credit score. When a borrower with only one or two trade lines receives a high score, it's not an accurate reflection of their limited credit history. Second, when a high-risk borrower can prove that he's paid multiple creditors in the past, it validates the lender's decision to finance the mortgage.

Yet some investors made us scratch our heads and question their thinking. For example, RFC required five trade lines, but their definition of what made a trade line acceptable was different from that of other investors. They allowed collections and charge-offs to be counted as trade lines as long as one trade line was either a revolving or installment account. If a borrower had a Target charge card with a $100 maximum credit limit and four collection accounts, he met the minimum requirement. Here's the craziest part. If the same borrower had a 580 credit score, he qualified for 100 percent financing.

So how does paying on a Target charge card qualify a borrower to purchase a home with no money down? The answer lies in the belief that credit score could accurately predict a loan's performance. While working at RFC, I attended a meeting in which a member of the risk department provided an analysis on the company's entire book of business. His report showed a near-perfect relationship between delinquencies and credit score. As credit score went down, delinquencies went up.

This fundamental belief changed the way the industry operated. By 2000, subprime investors used credit score as the primary determinant for assessing risk. Even so, most of them believed the other credit elements—housing history, bankruptcies, foreclosures, and collections—should meet the guidelines in order for credit score to be a reliable indicator. Holding these other factors constant was a critical part of the equation. One of the greatest mistakes made in the mortgage industry occurred around 2005 when many of these guidelines started to loosen, allowing more unqualified borrowers to get approved.

How Creative Financing Works

The following case studies show how loans that didn't initially qualify were massaged to improve the borrower's credit grade. Although each case study focuses on one or two elements to make it easier to digest, the majority of subprime loans required the use of multiple techniques to qualify borrowers.

Case Study One—Massaging Credit

Steve and Cassie Hodge are purchasing a home. He manages a restaurant and she works as a hairdresser. Since Cassie had a baby a year ago, she has been working only part-time, and because she is paid in cash she can't prove her income. They have little money in savings but Steve's parents have agreed to give them 5 percent toward a down payment.

Steve went through a bad divorce a few years ago and his ex-wife ran up charges on their credit cards, which left him with bills he couldn't pay. The resulting collection and charge-off accounts have negatively impacted his credit—his score is 520. Cassie's score is 600, but she has limited credit with only three trade lines reporting—two collection accounts and a Visa card.

Here is how credit scores are used in subprime lending. If two borrowers are proving income (a full doc loan), the lender uses the primary breadwinner's score to determine the credit grade. In this case, Steve makes the most money so the lender would use his score. For a stated income loan, the lender uses whichever score is lower. To maximize the credit grade, most stated loans only list the borrower with the highest score, and the other person is left off the application. A stated income loan for this couple would be written only for Cassie since her score is higher.

Steve qualifies for the loan based on just his income, but the challenge is the down payment. With a 520 credit score, the lender requires 15 percent, which leaves them 10 percent short. Cassie's 600 credit score qualifies her for a stated income loan with 5 percent down, but she has limited credit. For her credit score to be valid she needs five trade lines, which leaves her short by two accounts.

In either case, they don't qualify. To make this deal work, they need more money, better credit, or both.

Option A—Credit Repair

Steve and Cassie are in luck. They've chosen a savvy loan originator who works closely with a local credit repair company. As the name implies, these firms help consumers repair or improve their credit.

After six weeks of work, the company increases Steve's credit score by 40 points. At 560, he's eligible to purchase with 5 percent down, but there's another problem—the lender wants proof that timely rental payments have been made. In this case, they'll only accept copies of cancelled checks or a verification of rent (VOR) form completed by a management company as proof. Since parents, relatives, or friends who double as landlords will lie to help out, private VORs are not as reliable. While many subprime lenders accepted them, others wanted more dependable proof for borrowers classified as a higher risk.

The problem is for the last year they've been living rent-free with Cassie's father. Looking for any possible solution, the broker discovers her father owns a one-person consulting firm, STM Inc. This gives him an idea. He supplies the lender with a rental verification using STM as the property management company. The broker thinks a generic name like STM might just fool the lender. Even if the lender calls to verify the document, they'll end up talking with Cassie's dad, who'll verify its authenticity.

Why Is This an Issue?

From a lender's perspective, credit repair companies present a dichotomy. For borrowers who've had their identities stolen or need to challenge legitimate credit issues, they provide a much-needed service. In most cases, however, the service is the mortgage equivalent of cosmetic surgery. Using the tricks of the trade, they give Steve's credit report a face-lift, making it look better than it is. Artificially raising his score doesn't make him a better risk, it means he gets a loan with better terms.

Because Steve's housing history is altered, the lender can't accurately assess his credit profile. Since rental history is the one debt that best resembles a mortgage payment, it's a critical piece of information required to validate a lending decision for high-risk borrowers. When the VOR is manipulated, the final assessment is based on a flawed assumption.

Since their credit is poor, Steve and Cassie are more likely to default on a mortgage than someone with better credit. Requiring them to have more skin in the game by putting 15 percent down instead of only 5 percent is how the industry manages risk. If high-risk borrowers don't have as much to lose, their likelihood of walking away when times get tough goes up. This partially explains why this country is faced with record levels of foreclosures, as a large percentage of borrowers were financed with little or no money down.

Option B—Credit Enhancement

Instead of taking several months to repair Steve's credit, the broker opts for another strategy—credit enhancement. This is one of the newer tricks developed by the credit repair industry. A person with good credit is paid a fee for each account they let someone else use. The person with the challenged credit doesn't get access to the account, just the benefit of the performance history that comes with it.

You'll recall that Cassie couldn't qualify for a stated income loan because she didn't meet the five-trade-line requirement. Thanks to the credit enhancement process, three new trade lines are added to her credit report, which increases the score to 665. Because she had limited credit from the outset, doubling her total number of accounts significantly increases the score.

Her improved credit score creates two benefits. First, she qualifies for 100 percent financing under the stated income program. Second, because the score is now above 640, the rental verification becomes less of a concern. In this case a private VOR is considered acceptable by the lender. Not only can they qualify with no money down and no income verification, her father doesn't have to lie for them.

Why Is This an Issue?

From a risk perspective, credit enhancement is smoke and mirrors, a total facade. Nothing about the loan makes sense. The lender uses Cassie's credit to make a risk-based decision, but she has no ability to make the payments. Steve can make the payments, but his credit score is 100 points lower than hers and he's not on the application. This deal is based entirely on false assumptions.

Let's change the scenario and assume credit enhancement wasn't necessary. Cassie had the necessary depth of credit and was able to qualify with 5 percent down using a stated income program. What's been described so far has been a process driven by the broker. However, the lender's account executive often played a key role in structuring difficult deals.

The broker is looking to the lender's account executive for guidance. When it comes to configuring deals, the account executive will tell the broker how to package them so they get approved. A loan must be structured properly before it gets to the underwriting department or it will be denied. If a broker submits a stated income loan and includes a borrower's W-2 by mistake, most lenders won't allow the deal to go through because they've seen the income. If the loan is sent this way to a lender's account executive, he'll pull out the income documents, send it to underwriting, and the problem is solved. It's the account executive's responsibility to make certain the broker gets it right the first time.

Like brokers, account executives work mostly on commission, which means they don't get paid unless the deal closes. With the exception of Accredited Home Lenders, I don't know of any other mortgage company that tied loan-level risk factors, such as a stated income loan versus one with full documentation, to an account executive's commission structure. It was a brilliant model. By effectively giving the reps a financial interest in the quality of the loans they obtained, it motivated them to act in the best interest of the company. The majority of other lenders, however, paid their reps more money for higher margin products like subprime, which did nothing to prevent irresponsible behavior. Not surprisingly, the highest producing reps were usually the most creative.

Case Study Two—Leveraging Income

The Ortegas need 100 percent financing to purchase their first home. Both have strong job histories and make good income. Javier managed a local computer repair company for four years until he was recruited away last month by another firm. His promotion to regional manager resulted in a substantial pay increase from $55,000 to $100,000.

For five years, Wendy has managed the local chapter of a large non-profit, and she currently makes $95,000 a year. Javier's credit score is 615, and Wendy's is 555.

Option A—Guideline versus Practice

The industry guideline for calculating income is to average the most recent two years' W-2s and two pay stubs within the last 30 days. Using this approach, Javier's income is $77,500. Since Wendy makes more money, the lender uses her 555 score to qualify them. With only $3,000 in savings, they can't meet the required 10 percent down payment.

The industry practice, however, is to use the most recent W-2 and one pay stub within the last 60 days or use the borrower's current salary. In this case, Javier's income is $100,000, which makes him the primary wage earner. Since the lender will use his 615 credit score to qualify the loan, they're now eligible for 100 percent financing.

Why Is This an Issue?

This practice is common to both prime and subprime lending. When a salaried borrower's income rises, the new amount is used for qualification purposes. On the surface, this approach seems to make sense—if a person has improved his position in life he should be allowed to use the higher figure.

The guideline, however, exists for a reason. Part of the decision to lend money is based on how a borrower performs over time. Whether it's paying bills, making money, or holding down a job, each of these factors into a lender's decision. Though Javier is credited with making $100,000 a year, there's no track record to support this income.

Using the industry practice has different implications depending on the type of borrower. A consumer with excellent credit has a history of paying on time. This record helps offset the increased risk from giving someone greater buying power. The subprime borrower hasn't shown this kind of discipline. In many cases, there are no compensating factors to offset the increased risk.

What does this new buying power mean to the Ortegas? With a combined annual income of $195,000, they can qualify for a $750,000 mortgage. On a two-year ARM at 8 percent, the monthly principal and interest payment alone is $5,466. With taxes and insurance it goes to $6,700. If the interest rate adjusts to 10 percent a few years from now, the payment increases another $1,000 a month.

As an industry, mortgage lending is responsible for two things: effectively managing risk and minimizing the chance that consumers do something stupid. Using this method to calculate a subprime borrower's income doesn't serve either purpose. Of course, the Ortegas are responsible for putting themselves in this position. No one put a gun to their heads and told them to sign the loan documents. But the industry did nothing to stop it. In fact, the opposite happened. Applying whichever method was needed to increase a borrower's buying power, the industry practice or the guideline, was a reckless form of risk management.

Option B—Remove the Borrower with the Lower Credit Score

Let's assume Javier's income only increased to $85,000, making Wendy the primary wage earner. Using her 555 score, the lender requires a 10 percent down payment. Assuming the Ortegas were willing to buy a less expensive home, they could still qualify for 100 percent financing by just using his income. This means removing Wendy from the application so the lender can use his score. It gives them less buying power but enables them to purchase a home with no money down.

The deal is still being massaged to fit their needs, but at least it's a better lending decision. By using only his income, the maximum they can borrow is $300,000. Even though Wendy was removed from the loan application, the deal has a significant compensating factor—her income. She may not be signing on the note, but when her salary is factored into the equation, the payment becomes more reasonable. Compared to the initial scenario, which allowed them to maximize their buying power, it's a better risk for the borrower and the lender.

Why Is This an Issue?

The practice of removing a borrower from the loan application to get better terms happens frequently in subprime. These two options are contrasted to show how the business changed over the last seven years. In the early part of the decade, consumers seemed less inclined to push deals to the absolute limit. But when rates dropped and housing mania replaced all rational thinking, subprime lenders became the crack dealers of the financial industry—pedaling easy money to anyone who needed it. With a lending environment that promoted irresponsible behavior, borrowers threw caution to the wind and structured more loans that resembled the first scenario discussed for the Ortegas.

Case Study Three—It's All About What You Don't Tell Them . . .

Jenny Griffin owns a local bakery that makes unique custom cakes and pastries. Like most self-employed business owners, she uses her expenses to reduce her taxable income. Even though her business does well, her tax returns show very little income. Fortunately, the subprime industry has a 24-month bank-statement program that counts her deposits and treats them like income. Totaling the deposits for the last two years and dividing by 24 months will determine her average monthly income. This gives her the same buying power as qualifying with two years of tax returns.

Looking at the bank statements, the broker notices some problems. First, Jenny bounced a couple of checks last year when business slowed. Guidelines dictate that NSF (non-sufficient funds) or overdrafts are cause for immediate decline under the bank statement program. Second, she made a $25,000 deposit 14 months ago after winning a small Texas Hold'em tournament in Las Vegas. Anomalies like large deposits or balance transfers are excluded when calculating average income. If the underwriter doesn't count this deposit, Jenny's income will be too low to qualify.

Option A—Being Resourceful

Fortunately, the lender's account executive knows a few things the broker doesn't. In reviewing the statements, he noticed her deposits were greater during the most recent 12 months than the previous year. After crunching the numbers, he determines her income is high enough to qualify using just one year's bank statements. The broker didn't know the lender had a 12-month bank statement program through a different investor. Using this program, Jenny gets around the issue of the large deposit since it happened over a year ago.

The rep also knows how to get around the bounced checks. The guidelines require every page from the bank statements be submitted to underwriting. The common practice is only to provide the first page from each month's statement. This page displays a summary of her activity including total monthly deposits. To find the NSF, the underwriter has to search through a hundred pages of bank statements, which no one has time for. To expedite the process, most investors accept the front pages and never ask for the others, so the bounced checks go unnoticed.

Why Is This an Issue?

Admittedly, bouncing a check is not a heinous infraction. It's a mistake that can happen to even the most credit savvy consumers. But if Jenny bounced checks every month, which would make her a greater risk, she still could have been approved for the loan. It raises the question, "What good is a policy if no one adheres to it?"

In many ways this example resembles the last case study. Just as Javier Ortega was given credit for his newly increased salary, Jenny Griffin's underwriter is only using 12 months of income to determine the likelihood that she'll make her payments. For a self-employed borrower who poses a higher risk, it's an aggressive lending policy.

The bank statement program could also be manipulated in other ways. Let's assume the NSF showed up on the first page of a monthly statement. If Jenny could qualify using the other 11 statements while still dividing the total deposits by 12 months, the broker would submit the loan but omit the statement. As long as the calculations worked, the underwriter would approve the loan.

Case Study Four—Now You See It, Now You Don't

The mortgage industry uses a standard approach to determine which credit score is used for qualification purposes. First, for a borrower's score to be valid, a minimum of two credit bureaus must produce scores. In most cases, the bureaus are unable to produce a score if a borrower has little or no credit history. A complete credit report will include scores from all three repositories (Equifax, TransUnion, and Experian), but as long as two scores are produced a borrower can still qualify. Second, lenders will use either the middle of three scores or the lower of two scores as the qualifying number.

Bill and Rita Watson are purchasing a home, but they've got a problem. Their car was repossessed nine months ago, resulting in a $25,000 collection account. Since it's a large balance and occurred recently, investors require it to be paid off as a condition of the mortgage. In most cases, this isn't feasible, which means the deal gets denied. However, the lender's account executive notices the collection agency handling the account reports only to Equifax. Some small and midsized creditors will report to only one or two repositories in order to reduce costs. If the broker reissues the credit report but removes Equifax, producing information from only the other two bureaus, the collection disappears. One minute the account is there and the next it's gone. When the underwriter reviews the loan, she has no idea it ever existed.

Why Is This an Issue?

This is a radical example of how to manipulate credit. It has no redeeming value aside from approving borrowers for a loan they didn't qualify for, the subprime equivalent of three-card monte.

Dropping borrowers from the application or removing bureaus from a credit report was a manipulative process. Here are some other examples in which this method was used to qualify borrowers:

- The Watsons have a large car payment that's preventing them from qualifying. Since the debt was reported to only one bureau, the broker drops that bureau from the borrower's credit report and the debt disappears. The underwriter is unable to accurately determine the borrower's debt-to-income ratio.
- If a debt or collection account that prevents the Watsons from qualifying is in only one of their names, the lender drops that person from the application. If the remaining borrower doesn't make enough money to qualify on his or her own, the lender puts that person into a stated income loan.

Using this tactic requires a certain amount of luck to be successful. Whenever a repository or borrower is dropped from a deal, it's possible the loan will get worse, not better. If the dropped repository has the highest of the three scores, the borrower ends up with a lower score since the lender uses the lower of the two remaining scores versus the middle of the original three scores. With a lower credit score, the borrower's grade could go down, which would require a larger down payment. It's fortunate that a large percentage of creditors report to all three repositories; otherwise subprime lending could approve substantially more unqualified borrowers.

Case Study Five—Automated Underwriting

The widespread use of automated underwriting (AU) technology brought subprime lending into the twenty-first century. Although systems were slow to develop, most lenders had some form of AU technology in place by 2004. The more robust systems used risk-based decision-making that went beyond basic underwriting guidelines. If a borrower's compensating factors warranted a loan exception, the best systems could make that call.

They also helped remove the guesswork. With AU approval, a broker had something more tangible to tell his borrower and his realtor. Since lenders stood behind their systems, an approval all but guaranteed a loan would fund. As long as the property value could be substantiated and the information on the application could be verified, loans would close.

AU systems not only modernized the subprime industry, they helped address the greatest frustration for lenders and brokers—scores that declined because lenders had reordered credit reports. Before automation, most brokered loans underwent a similar process. The broker sent a loan application and credit report to his account executive for prequalification. Let's assume the borrower had a 590 credit score and was preapproved for 100 percent financing. When the loan arrived at the lender's office three weeks later, the lender ordered a new credit report, which is standard operating procedure. In this case, the score dropped to 550. Since the lender used their scores to underwrite the loan, the borrower was no longer eligible for 100 percent financing. With no cash available for a down payment, the deal quickly fell apart.

AU technology solved this problem. When a broker used a lender's AU system, he could utilize his credit report to get the approval. Once the loan file arrived at the lender's office, the underwriter would access the system and print out the broker's credit report in the lender's name. The issue of falling credit scores became a thing of the past.

Why Is This an Issue?

When a credit score drops, it means one of three things:

1. The borrower was recently late on a payment.
2. He has used more of his total available credit by running up his credit cards.
3. He has applied for new credit.

When any or all of these happen, the borrower becomes a greater credit risk, which causes his score to deteriorate.

Most investors considered credit reports to be valid for 60 days. This meant a loan had two months to close from the date the credit report was issued, otherwise a new report had to be ordered. Some investors were more aggressive. Credit reports issued through Assetwise, RFC's AU system, were valid for 120 days. Although it provided lenders with a great selling tool, this may have been the single worst risk policy implemented in the history of RFC. The 60-day time limit has a purpose. High-risk borrowers are less responsible than prime borrowers when it comes to managing their credit. Allowing them 120 days between the time credit is ordered and a loan is closed is long enough to have every account go to collection, file for bankruptcy, get divorced, and have time to spare.

This credit policy created a Catch-22. With RFC, when a broker's credit report being used through Assetwise was more than 60 days old, we usually pulled credit again to be certain nothing drastic had happened to the borrower. When the credit score dropped significantly, it left us with two choices: decline the loan and upset the broker by not standing behind the AU system, or close a mortgage for a borrower who no longer qualified. To save face with our customer and remain competitive, we usually chose the latter.

For all the benefits AU technology brought to subprime lending, one thing is clear—automation helped lenders close loans that should have been declined. Eight years ago the issue of falling credit scores was a common occurrence in subprime lending. Until automation became a standard part of the business, 10 to 15 percent of loans that brokers submitted to underwriting were turned down for this reason. Getting an AU approval for loans that should have been denied didn't make the borrowers creditworthy—it meant technology had found a way to circumvent the issue.

Appraisals

Property valuation is a highly subjective process. Ask two residential real estate appraisers to assess a property's value and you'll likely get two different answers. Pose the same question to the consumer, broker, lender, and investor, and you'll get four more. When it comes to valuing real estate, everyone has an opinion. While the most important judgment belongs to the appraiser, it's by no means the most reliable.

As impartial evaluators, appraisers are supposed to remain objective, following a set of rules and guidelines to determine a property's fair market value. Their opinion shouldn't be influenced by anything other than the available data in the marketplace. This is a case where theory and reality are seldom in sync.

Appraisers rely on the lenders and brokers who hire them to make a living. Being true to their profession and pleasing the customer is a difficult balancing act. When a broker orders an appraisal, he provides an estimate or target value for the property to the appraiser. If the appraiser has problems consistently reaching this number, the broker will hire someone else. Any appraiser who goes strictly by the book can struggle to get repeat business.

Since property valuation is subjective, there's an acceptable fudge factor for appraising real estate. This is an allowable deviation—an amount or percentage a property's appraised value can vary from what a lender or investor thinks it is worth.

Allowing brokers to choose the appraiser, combined with the fudge factor, created a system that was vulnerable to abuse. As commissioned salespeople with no vested interest in a loan's performance, brokers have the means and the motive to influence the final appraised value. Since the influence is very real and subprime lenders know it, they'll come to view any broker-ordered appraisal with a high degree of skepticism.

Why is value so critical to the broker? If a home is under contract for $250,000 but it appraises for only $240,000, the deal is in jeopardy. The lender uses the lower of the purchase price or the appraised value as the final home value for lending purposes. If the seller isn't willing to drop the sales price to meet the appraised value, the buyer needs to bring in the difference ($10,000) in addition to whatever funds were already required for the down payment and closing costs. For cash-strapped subprime borrowers, this usually kills the deal.

Case Study Six—How to Fudge a Little

A broker orders an appraisal indicating the target property value is $325,000. The borrower wants to refinance and get as much cash as possible. The appraiser's initial look-up shows comparable sales (comps) in the area range from $278,000 to $362,000. At first glance, the target value appears reasonable.

An appraiser should use comps that best resemble the subject property in age, size, style, and location. While appraisers should use a minimum of three comps, they can have more depending on what has sold in the area over the last six months. If the selection is thin, the appraiser will search for the nearest comps that most closely resemble the subject. The appraiser modifies the value for each comp relative to the subject property by adjusting up or down for major factors—square footage, number of bedrooms and bathrooms, swimming pool, and so on. This helps the appraiser determine a fair market value for the property.

In this example, we'll assume the property values have already been adjusted for these factors. For this loan, the appraiser finds four comps with the following values:

$290,000

$299,000

$308,000

$311,000

At first glance, it doesn't appear the target value of $325,000 is supported using these comps. So the appraiser digs a little deeper and finds two additional comps a mile away with values of $335,000 and $343,000. He also realizes that just adding them into the mix won't support the target value unless he removes the two lowest comps. After

determining they weren't as representative of the subject as he originally thought (too small, too old, wrong style), he feels justified in removing them. These are the four comps he uses for the appraisal:

$308,000

$311,000

$335,000

$343,000

This produces a final value of $325,000. Having followed his profes-
sional standards, he believes it accurately represents the property's fair
market value. This process shows that stretching an appraised value by
5 to 10 percent is not difficult. However, the difference between creativity and manipulation is a fine line that's open to interpretation.

Knowing that property values are often stretched, lenders develop a
routine to validate the appraiser's work. Most start by checking county
tax records and using one or more automated valuation models
(AVMs). These programs provide basic information on properties in
the area that sold, including square footage, date of sale, and distance
from subject property.

The AVM shows 18 sales in the area over the last six months. However, only three properties sold above the $325,000 appraised value,
two of which were used as comps. This is a telltale sign the appraiser is
stretching the value. Sometimes looking at the property photos can provide more information. Not surprisingly, the two higher-priced comps
appear nicer than the subject property. In fact, the subject property
more closely resembles the other two comps ($308,000 and $311,000).
If the lender's assumptions are correct, the property is overvalued by
$15,000, making it worth closer to $310,000. It's clear the appraiser is
using some of his fudge factor to reach the target value.

At this stage, the lender either accepts the value or does more research. If they believe the deviation is small, they might order a desk review. This means another appraiser reviews the original work without
going to the property. As the name implies, he will conduct the review
from a desk, only using whatever AVMs are at his disposal. If the lender

is uncomfortable with the original appraisal, they'll order a field review. This is more extensive and requires the new appraiser to visit the property, examine the original appraiser's work, and provide additional comps if necessary.

In this case, the lender accepts the value without any additional reviews. The borrower refinances 100 percent of the appraised value, which means he's probably borrowing $15,000 more than the property is worth. The lender and the investor sign off on the loan, believing the variance is reasonable. Although the industry had no published standard, five years of funding and selling subprime mortgages told us at Kellner that 10 percent was an acceptable deviation for our four investors: Countrywide, RFC, Household, and Citi. This means that if the investor's underwriter thought the property was worth $310,000, they'd accept an appraised value up to $341,000. Anything above this threshold ran the risk of being declined. Ten percent may not sound like much, but as you'll read in a moment, this variance was a major reason property values increased as much as they did.

How to Fudge a Lot

Let's assume the scenario is different. In this case, the borrower has more debt to pay, which requires the broker to give the appraiser a higher target value. Since the borrower is trying to pay two collections, a federal tax lien, and get $25,000 in cash, the broker determines a $359,000 value is required to pay all the bills and pay his two-point commission. This figure is $34,000 higher than the original targeted value of $325,000. So instead of using the four comps, the appraiser keeps the highest one and discards the others. To increase the appraised value, he goes north three miles and finds two new comps, one for $359,000 and another for $363,000. He adds a fourth comp for $372,000, located three miles northwest. These are the four comps:

$343,000

$359,000

$363,000

$372,000

The appraiser submits a $359,000 property value to the lender. Compared to $310,000, which was the lender's original estimated value, it's a 15 percent deviation.

One look at the area map reveals the appraiser's tactics. The subject property is located in a midsize city, just south of downtown. Getting from it to any of the new comps requires driving across a major highway and two sets of railroad tracks to a nicer part of town. The appraiser found more affluent neighborhoods and used these comps to stretch the value. The property photos confirm that the new comps are much nicer than the subject. Since the lender recognizes the appraiser's strategy, he'll order a field review. Not surprisingly, the reviewer cuts the value by $40,000, providing the lender with four new comps to support a value of $319,000.

Even a loan with a deviation this large could work, it just requires some creativity. While the lender believes the field reviewer's assessment is accurate, this value won't work because the collections and tax lien must be paid, and the broker has informed the lender that if the borrower doesn't get some cash at closing, he won't close the loan. So the lender counters with a value of $341,000, which is a full 10 percent deviation from the original value of $310,000. To get the borrower some more cash, the broker eliminates his two-point origination fee but increases the interest rate by 1.25 percent to make it back in a yield-spread premium.

The final value is not arbitrary. It's derived by knowing exactly how far a value can be fudged and by working all the numbers down to the last penny. In the end, the borrower gets what he wanted, the lender and broker each earn a premium, and the investor received a performing loan.

There's one problem with this example. The property must appreciate substantially for the borrower to break even when the time comes to sell. In an up market like 2001 to 2004, he might have gotten away with it. But if this loan closed in the last few years, especially in an inflated market like Las Vegas, Phoenix, or Miami, the borrower is in a world of hurt.

Understanding the Impact

Subprime lenders used to conduct a desk or field review for most broker-ordered appraisals because these appraisals were considered to be unreliable. For us, the number of unreliables reached as high as 80 percent. With the appraisal process highly susceptible to manipulation, lenders had to conduct business as though the broker and appraiser couldn't be trusted. This meant that either the majority of appraisers were incompetent or they were influenced by brokers to increase the value. Brokers didn't need to exert direct influence. Instead they picked another appraiser until someone consistently delivered the results they needed.

To put things in perspective, there's nothing extreme about the example given in Case Study Six. During my company's history, half of all the loans we underwrote were overvalued by as much as 10 percent. This meant one out of two appraisals was still within an acceptable tolerance for our end investors. Another quarter were overvalued by 11 to 20 percent. These loans were either declined or the value reduced to an acceptable level. The remaining quarter were so overvalued they defied all logic. Throwing a dart at a board while blindfolded would have produced more accurate results. The excessive inflation of property values largely explains why subprime loans experienced a high rate of decline.

The implications become evident from doing the math. If multiple properties in an area are overvalued by 10 percent, they become comps for future appraisals. The process then repeats itself. We saw it on several occasions. We'd close a loan in January and see the subject property show up as a comp in the same neighborhood six months later. Except this time, the new subject property, which was nearly identical in size and style to the home we financed in January, was being appraised for 10 percent more. Of course, demand is a key component to driving value, but the defective nature of the appraisal process served as an accelerant. In the end, the subprime industry's willingness to consistently accept overvalued appraisals significantly contributed to the run-up in property values experienced throughout the country.

How is this possible when a home or any asset should be worth whatever the market will bear? The answer lies with the down payment. If similar homes in an area have sold for $350,000, and a seller gets a contract for $400,000, that's a function of market demand. A home is worth whatever someone is willing to pay for it. The appraisal, however, should still show that the property is valued at only $350,000. Since there are no comparable sales to justify the higher sales price, lenders should base the loan amount on the $350,000 value, not the $400,000 purchase price. If a borrower wishes to buy the home at a premium price, he must bring an additional $50,000 in cash to closing, the difference between the purchase price and the appraised value.

If the process had worked correctly, a significant percentage of subprime borrowers would have been turned down due to a lack of funds. Inevitably, this would have forced sellers to drop their exorbitant asking prices to more reasonable levels. The rate of property appreciation experienced on a national basis over the last seven years was not only a function of market demand but was due, in part, to the subprime industry's acceptance of overvalued appraisals, coupled with a high percentage of credit-challenged borrowers who financed with no money down.

Laying the Blame

So who is responsible for this fiasco? Everyone from the broker and the appraiser to the lender and the investor shares in the blame, even though no industry group is willing to take responsibility. Why should they? Doing so equates to self-incrimination.

For me, the issue of property valuation served as a major source of frustration. Sandwiched between brokers who had no liability, an appraisal industry that was inherently flawed, and investors who were willing to buy loans with inflated appraisals, there's no question the entire process was defective. While every lender who closed a loan with an overvalued appraisal bears some responsibility, the issues we experienced led me to believe there was a much larger problem.

When Kellner first opened, we used several different appraisal evaluation companies to conduct our desk and field reviews. Since we didn't order the initial appraisals, these reviews played an important part in helping us make our final lending decision. If a review appraiser confirmed our suspicion that a property was overvalued, we either cut the property value to an acceptable level or denied the loan. Conversely, if we suspected an appraisal was overvalued but the review appraiser confirmed it was correct, we took this into consideration when making our decision. After all, an appraisal is just an opinion. Just because we suspect a property is overvalued doesn't mean we're correct. If both the original appraiser and the review appraiser are in agreement, we're going to rely on their collective judgment as licensed professionals to make the right call.

A year after we opened, we decided to order all appraisal reviews through Landsafe, a wholly owned subsidiary of Countrywide Credit Industries, because of the tie-in between their two companies. If a loan was sent to Countrywide for purchase and Landsafe performed the appraisal or the appraisal review, Countrywide agreed to accept whatever property value Landsafe determined was accurate. It was a brilliant business strategy. Since determining property value was so critical to the lending process, their commitment to stand behind Landsafe provided us with security. It didn't matter if we thought an appraisal was overvalued by 20 percent—if Landsafe blessed it, Countrywide treated it as gospel. They never put it in writing, and sometimes it took a little arm-twisting when values were questionable, but they stood behind their commitment.

The problem started whenever Countrywide made Kellner repurchase a loan, usually due to fraud on the part of the broker. When an investor issued a repurchase request, either the lender paid cash for the note or both parties agreed to a settlement based on an estimated loss. This required taking into consideration the property value, loan amount, premium paid to the lender, as well as a host of other costs. Smaller lenders, like Kellner, preferred to create a settlement since it meant not having to use large sums of cash to buy back the loans.

Since the property value was supported by a Landsafe appraisal review, it seems reasonable that Countrywide would use the same value when calculating a settlement. Somehow logic never made it into the equation. Instead, Countrywide would order a broker price opinion (BPO)—an independent third-party appraisal to determine a new property value. In every instance, which amounted to more than a dozen repurchase requests over a four-year period, the BPO Countrywide received was substantially lower than Landsafe's value, in some cases by as much as 20 to 25 percent.

Trying to reason with their repurchase department was pointless. Our conversations bordered on nonsensical as we listened to them justify why Landsafe's opinion was not acceptable to them, even though they owned the company. The justification they used was that Landsafe's value only applied to the front end of their business.

Tying the use of Landsafe's appraisal services to Countrywide's core business paid enormous dividends. They not only made money off the appraisal fee income, they bought more loans from lenders as a result of the tie-in. For Kellner, purchasing a Landsafe appraisal review was like buying an insurance policy that only paid when it served Countrywide's financial interest. Once the loan became a liability, Landsafe went from being a member of the Countrywide family to being the redheaded stepchild.

By accepting the BPO instead of Landsafe's opinion, Countrywide sent the message that Landsafe was wrong. If this happened once, twice, or even a few times, I'd chalk it up to an overzealous appraiser. But since the property value for every repurchase request was dramatically reduced, there are only three possible conclusions. First, every Landsafe appraiser was incompetent, which seems unlikely since all of them were licensed professionals. Second, Countrywide influenced the appraisers conducting the BPOs to produce overly conservative estimates in order to reduce their losses. This is possible but also unlikely since these appraisers worked independent of Countrywide. Third, Countrywide encouraged Landsafe appraisers to validate excessive property values.

To an outsider, the last option might not make any sense. Why would any lender, let alone the largest mortgage company in the United States, implement such a practice? Since all lenders have a financial interest in the loan's performance, endorsing excessive property values is tantamount to playing with fire.

If you understand how the process worked, however, the logic behind the practice becomes clear. Even if a property was overvalued, there was no immediate concern to Countrywide as long as the loan paid on time. Once a loan became delinquent, Countrywide's QC department tore it apart looking for any reason a lender should be required to repurchase the mortgage. Of course, just because a loan was delinquent didn't mean it would become a repurchase, but many of them did. Once a repurchase request was triggered, the loss ultimately moved from Countrywide's balance sheet to another lender.

If Landsafe endorsed overvalued appraisals on the front side, it drove more business, which created more profit. Disregarding Landsafe's opinion on the backside enabled them to minimize some of the losses. The strategy worked well as long as the status quo didn't change. When the meltdown that became the mortgage Armageddon of 2007 didn't leave any subprime lenders to absorb the losses, Countrywide was left holding the bag.

The important question is just how much the issue of overvalued appraisals will impact Countrywide over the next few years. If my experience in any way resembles the standards used by Landsafe in Countrywide's other divisions, the next 12 to 24 months will prove to be painful for America's #1 home loan lender. It also means that their projected return to profitability in 2008 will be nothing short of fantasy.

CHAPTER 5

Wall Street and the Rating Agencies: Greed at Its Worst

U ntil now, we've focused on the front end of the business by discussing the people who made the loans and the tactics they used to qualify challenging borrowers. Let's shift our attention to the back side of the industry and what happens to a mortgage once it has closed and funded. We'll examine how mortgage securitization works and analyze the Wall Street investment firms that drove the process as well as the agencies that rated the securities. These participants, in my opinion, share the greatest blame for the current housing fiasco.

A lender's ability to function depends on the existence of a secondary market. While banks and large financial institutions have sufficient capital to fund and hold mortgages in portfolio, most lenders don't have that capability. A secondary market provides an outlet for lenders to sell mortgages, pay off their warehouse lines of credit, make a profit, and start the process over again. Without it, only the most highly capitalized companies could operate as mortgage lenders.

Our examination of the mortgage securitization process, the investment firms, and the rating agencies will lead to some troubling conclusions.

- The relationship between the investment firms and rating agencies was fundamentally flawed, which compromised the rating process.

- Investors who purchased these mortgage-backed securities believed they were investment grade, when in fact the risk was much greater.

- Since the secondary market dictated the products lenders could offer, investment firms and rating agencies became the unofficial regulators of the subprime industry.

- The securitization market transformed the U.S. mortgage market, in some ways to the detriment of the consumer.

The Impact of Securitization

Securitization could be the single greatest innovation in mortgage lending. Before loans were securitized, a consumer relied on a bank to supply the money to fund a mortgage. The entire process, from origination to servicing, stayed with the same institution. Since banks owned every aspect of the loan and were heavily regulated, they were motivated to manage risk and treat borrowers fairly. If a consumer got into financial trouble because of something like layoffs at a local factory, the local bank often knew about it before it became an issue. Owning the entire process gave banks the latitude to restructure the loan. You'll see later in this chapter how securitization negatively impacts a borrower's ability to modify his mortgage.

In addition to creating a renewable source of capital, mortgage securitization helped fragment the industry. A broker originated a loan while a mortgage lender funded it. The lender either sold the loan to another financial institution that held it in portfolio or used an investment bank to package it into a mortgage-backed security. A myriad of investors, ranging from banks to hedge funds, bought the investments for their portfolio. A servicing company collected payments, and when a loan defaulted, foreclosed on the property. The entire process originally performed by one entity was divided into five separate components.

This fragmentation gave each player a claim of plausible deniability. Mortgage brokers maintained that they only originated the loan, so any concerns about the loan's quality were the lender's responsibility. The lender underwrote the deal using the guidelines provided by the investment firms, so they merely delivered the final product investors wanted to buy. The Wall Street firms who packaged the securities and the investors who purchased them claimed to be "Holders in Due Course," which protected them from any liability when lenders and brokers acted illegally. The entire food chain contributed to the current problems, but fragmentation allowed each player to point an accusatory finger at someone else.

While there is plenty of blame to go around, one conclusion is difficult to refute. The problems in today's housing market exist because the investment banks packaged high-risk loans into securities and the rating agencies assessed them as investment quality. If the investors who purchased the securities understood what they were buying, the outcome would likely have been different.

Understanding Mortgage-Backed Securities

In Chapter 2 securitization was described as a process where thousands of mortgages are bundled together into financial products called mortgage-backed securities (MBS). The investors, usually banks or hedge funds, who purchase the bonds receive the principal and interest payments made by borrowers.

To show how it works, let's assume a Wall Street firm like Merrill Lynch has a $1 billion pool of subprime mortgages. To package these loans into a security requires the services of a rating agency. Companies like Moody's conduct an extensive analysis, determining the quality and performance characteristics for the entire pool of mortgages. The ratings they provide help the potential purchaser understand the risks associated with buying them.

The graphic in Figure 5.1 explains the basics of mortgage securitization. The security has levels or *tranches* (*tranche* is a French word for slice or section). In the financial sense of the word, each tranche is a piece of the deal's risk. As you move from the highest

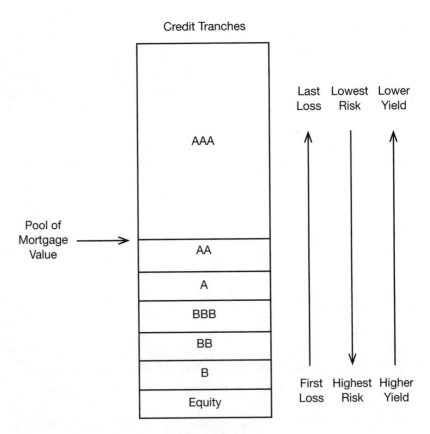

Figure 5.1   The Basics of Mortgage Securitization

rated slices of the security (AAA) to the lowest (Equity), the risk goes up, but so does the potential return.

Moody's reviews the pool of loans and determines that for 80 percent of a potential security to receive an AAA rating (making it investment grade), the other 20 percent has to be rated between AA and Equity. This format is commonly referred to as a senior-subordinate structure, meaning the lowest or subordinate tranches will sustain losses before the senior pieces. It also means the AAA investors get paid first, followed by AA, and so on. Purchasing the AAA portion of this security means that 20 percent of the entire pool must experience a loss before the AAA section is negatively impacted. The same way the pawns protect the king in chess, the lower tranches protect the higher tranches by taking the initial loss.

Here is where it gets more complicated. The security gets spliced and diced into a hodgepodge of separate investment vehicles—CMOs (collateralized mortgage obligations), CDOs (collateralized debt obligations), and CLOs (collateralized loan obligations), all of which represent different ways to distribute credit risk. The security gets diluted even further as some CDOs are backed by other CDOs, which can then invest again in other CDOs. We revisit CDOs toward the end of this chapter.

Since the original mortgages are no longer recognizable, judging the quality of the assets is next to impossible. Think of it this way: Imagine taking 10 different vegetables and pureeing them in a food processor until you have something close to soup. Ask someone to identify the ingredients but don't let him taste it—make him rely strictly on his sense of sight. Your concoction is sure to make him wonder what's inside.

Investors who buy these securities face the same challenge. Many believe the confusing nature of the investments means the fund managers who purchased them had no clue what they were buying. For this reason, the rating agencies are vital to the process. Without their objective analysis, investors wouldn't be able to recognize the risk associated with purchasing the securities.

Why is something as simple as a mortgage payment dissected into a myriad of investment options? In the 1980s, companies like Salomon Brothers and Drexel Burnham Lambert determined that mortgages were more valuable when spliced into pieces. It's similar to corporate raiders who buy companies on the cheap, break them up, and sell off the pieces. The sum of the parts is greater than the whole.

Wall Street Enters the Mix

Subprime was still in its infancy in the mid-1990s when Lehman Brothers became the first Wall Street investment bank to aggressively enter the business. Its earliest efforts to align with a subprime lender, however, proved disastrous.

In 1995, when they provided financing for First Alliance Mortgage Co. and underwrote the securities, Lehman's own internal memos questioned whether some borrowers had the capacity for repayment. As other investment banks backed away from First Alliance, federal and state regulators started to investigate their practices. Throughout the turmoil, Lehman continued to support First Alliance, keeping the operation in business. Even though Lehman internally acknowledged the potential for bad publicity as a result of their involvement, they stayed the course, believing the potential fee income outweighed the risks.

In 2003 a California jury awarded over $50 million in damages against First Alliance and attributed 10 percent of the responsibility to Lehman's involvement. It was eventually discovered that many of the sales tactics used by loan officers at First Alliance confused and misled borrowers. Viewing the experience with First Alliance as an aberration, Lehman was already pursuing other investment opportunities. One year before First Alliance closed its doors in 2000, Lehman, in a joint venture with then-ailing Amresco, Inc., became the first major Wall Street firm to operate a subprime lending unit, Finance America. The next year they acquired BNC Mortgage and eventually merged the two companies together.

In 2000, other Wall Street firms started to enter the subprime business. While some acquired servicing operations, others followed Lehman's example and purchased mortgage companies. Within a few years, major Wall Street firms like Merrill Lynch and Bear Stearns began acquiring subprime mortgages through multiple channels (wholesale and retail) to feed their securitization machines.

While lending firms made excellent profits, the big Wall Street firms made a killing. If you recall the profitability discussion from Chapter 2, imagine bypassing the middleman—companies like Kellner Mortgage who were getting paid 400 to 500 basis points—and taking mortgages from the consumer and broker levels and putting them directly into a security. The record earnings on Wall Street were driven, in part, by the mortgage securitization business. The high margin and the explosive housing market only fueled the desire for even more of this product.

Although Wall Street is skilled at making money, risk management has never been an area of expertise. This point can't be stressed enough: The current mortgage debacle is a direct result of Wall Street's inability to manage risk. In fact, companies like Merrill Lynch had no effective risk management processes in place until shortly before the subprime implosion. Since the focus was on feeding the securitization machine and driving profits, no one was paying attention to the basic fundamental principles of risk management.

The Rating Agencies

Until the 1970s, rating agencies operated under a business model different from the one they use today. An investor who wanted ratings bought a subscription to the agency's service. When the Securities and Exchange Commission (SEC) decided that the ratings serve a greater public interest, the SEC changed the business model. Instead of buying a subscription, companies would have to pay the agencies for rating their debt. In hindsight this may have been the single greatest mistake in the history of the SEC.

Except for those loans backed by the U.S. government, most mortgages are rated by one of three credit rating agencies: Moody's, Standard and Poor's (S&P), and Fitch. These companies evaluate the loss potential for a pool of mortgages. They examine everything from the expected frequency and severity of defaults to the characteristics of the loans within the security. Instead of examining every loan, they only use a sample, relying on the representations provided by the issuers.

Given the huge discrepancy between the performances of subprime mortgage-backed securities and the ratings they received, one or more of the following assertions seem plausible. First, the relationship between the investment firms and the agencies was compromised. Second, the investment firms provided the agencies with insufficient information to grade the securities accurately. This supports the agencies' belief that their ratings are only as good as the information given to them. Third, the statistical models the agencies used to evaluate the mortgage pools were defective. Each of these claims will be considered as the agency–Wall Street relationship is examined.

A Lucrative Business Model

Rating mortgage-backed securities is a highly profitable business. During the last five years, Moody's has been one of the most profitable companies in the S&P 500 stock index. Standard and Poor's and Fitch have generated phenomenal returns as well. As the real estate market soared, so did their income. When the Hearst Corporation purchased a 20 percent stake in Fitch in 2006, they viewed the income opportunities from rating CDOs as a highly attractive feature of the sale.

Before 2001, the agencies generated most of their income by rating corporate bonds. As the real estate market soared, income from rating mortgage-backed securities greatly exceeded their core business. According to figures provided by S&P spokesman Chris Atkins in an August 12, 2007, *Seattle Times* article, they charge nearly three times as much (12 basis points) to value a CDO as they do to rate a corporate bond (4.25 basis points). A $1 billion CDO generates $1.2 million in income. Moody's doesn't disclose its pricing schedule, but Fitch does. The gap between their fees charged for rating corporate bonds (3 to 7 basis points) and rating CDOs (7 to 8 basis points) is not as great as Standard and Poor's, but it's still significant.

Since $1 to $2 trillion in new residential mortgage-backed securities have been issued every year since 2002, the agencies had a strong motive to pursue this business. When you add up the figures, the numbers are staggering. Using a 10 basis-point average fee, $1 trillion in new securities issued equals $1 billion in revenue.

Unlike the lenders and investment firms, the rating agencies possess two advantages. First, since they're paid a percentage based on the size of the security, their income only changes relative to volume. In other words, while lenders and investment firms have at least some financial interest in the performance of a product, the agencies always get their cut. Second, even if they drastically misrepresent how a security should perform, they face no liability. If a baseball umpire consistently makes poor calls, the league replaces him. When an agency makes a bad call, an investment firm has no reason to use someone else. In fact, the opposite is true. Since agencies face no liability for inaccurate assessments, there is no advantage to being cautious. A liberal approach to rating securities means more profit for their Wall Street customers.

A Hand in the Process

As the official umpires in the world of big league finance, the agencies exist to provide the investment world with objective analyses. To understand the importance of their work, consider that many regulated financial institutions—insurance companies and banks—can only purchase investment-quality (AAA) debt. This means they can only put money into conservative, safe investments. Without the agencies, the financial institutions wouldn't know what qualifies as investment grade. Of course, all types of investors rely on the agencies' opinions, not just regulated industries.

The recent turmoil indicates, however, that rating agencies aren't objective. Josh Rosner, managing director of the research firm Graham Fisher, noted in an op-ed piece in the *New York Times* that raters play a significant role in assisting the issuers. He put it this way:

> The rating agencies are far from passive arbitrators in the markets. In structured finance, the rating agency can be an active part of the construction of the deal. In fact, the original models used to rate collateralized debt obligations were created in close cooperation with the investment banks that designed the securities.

The rating agencies liken themselves to information providers, claiming they have structures in place to prevent conflicts of interest. This is the corporate mantra but evidence suggests otherwise. Two colleagues, who asked not to be identified, have attended sales presentations given by the agencies. Both confirmed the agencies help clients structure complicated mortgage securities before they ever get rated. Using the agencies to guide them, investment firms package the securities to get a higher percentage of the MBSs rated as AAA. It's the equivalent of having a teacher write a student's term paper for him.

Why do investment firms want a higher percentage of the security rated AAA? The answer, like everything else in the mortgage industry, comes back to profit. Because of the reduced risk, the AAA tranche can be sold at a higher price than the lower tranches. Since the subordinated pieces carry more risk, they're sold at a discount. To maximize revenue, investment firms need the largest possible percentage of the security to receive an AAA rating.

As Rosner notes in the same op-ed piece, the system has problems:

Only slightly more than a handful of American non-financial corporations get the highest AAA rating, but almost 90% of collateralized debt obligations (CDOs) that receive a rating are bestowed such a title. Are we willing to believe that these securities are as safe as those of our most honored corporations?

To understand the significance of his statement requires a basic knowledge of CDOs. A CDO is nothing more than a redistribution of credit risk. It takes the lowest rated tranches from different securities and packages them together into a separate structure. Agencies rate a CDO the same way they do a mortgage-backed security, slicing it into AAA, AA, and so on.

If subprime lenders made chicken salad out of chicken shit, rating agencies turned it into filet mignon. To claim a subprime CDO carries the same risk as bonds issued by the most financially sound corporations is not only mind-boggling, it's negligent. With CDO losses reaching the billions, investors have retreated from buying all but the very safest of mortgage-backed securities.

A Conflicted Relationship

The entire rating process appears to be fundamentally flawed. By now, the inherent contradictions in the system should be clear on several levels. First, since the investment banks compensate the agencies, the relationship, in Rosner's words, is "hopelessly conflicted." Second, as active participants in the deals they structure, the agencies are not objective. Third, having no liability coupled with exorbitant revenues is a toxic combination.

There's another aspect to the relationship that merits discussion. If an investment bank issuing a security believes 80 percent of it should be rated AAA and the agency can validate only 75 percent, the issuer can threaten to move the business to another agency, but it doesn't usually come to that. Since the agencies understand the threat is real, they perform an advisory function to help their clients achieve the desired results.

In some ways, the investment firm-rating agency relationship mirrors the dysfunctional nature of the broker-lender relationship. If the broker is having trouble getting a deal approved, his account executive will tell him how to structure the loan. When an investment bank has a security filled with garbage loans, the agencies advise them how to structure the deals in order to maximize profit. A former analyst, who asked not to be identified, said, "the agencies understand the kind of pressure they're under to meet the expectations of Wall Street. If they didn't advise them, particularly on some of the tougher deals, the investment banks would struggle to hit their numbers."

The agencies defend themselves by issuing hundred-page disclaimers to go with the ratings. They emphasize that users of the information shouldn't rely on any credit rating or opinion within the analysis for making investment decisions.

Since the investment world depends on the agencies to provide impartial and objective evaluations, the disclaimers only serve to undermine the ratings. What good are they if investors can't rely on them? It's equivalent to building a car and sticking a label on the inside of a door that reads, "We want you to know we can't stand behind anyone who had anything to do with the assembly of this vehicle. If the steering wheel falls off, motor falls out, or any bodily injury comes to you as a result of driving this car, just remember, we told you so."

The Power of the Agencies

To understand just how powerful the rating agencies have become, consider this quote from *New York Times* columnist Thomas Friedman:

> There are two superpowers in the world today in my opinion. There's the United States and there's Moody's Bond Rating

Service. The United States can destroy you by dropping bombs, and Moody's can destroy you by downgrading your bonds. And believe me, it's not clear sometimes who's more powerful.

The power a company wields is best seen when its livelihood is threatened. The rating agencies proved their dominance in 2002 when Georgia passed a highly restrictive predatory lending law. The agencies determined that investors who purchased securities that contained certain types of loans could be held liable. To avoid this exposure, the agencies refused to rate any securities that contained these mortgages. Without an agency rating, investment banks couldn't securitize the loans, which meant lenders had no secondary market to buy them. The agencies effectively shut down the Georgia mortgage market, forcing legislators to amend the law. Strangely enough, for all the negative press targeted at subprime lenders, the rating agencies did more to inhibit predatory lending legislation than any other group.

The agencies believed the original Georgia law was in direct conflict with the Holder in Due Course doctrine. This principle protects the secondary market investors who purchase mortgage notes by immunizing them from liability. For example, a person who's been victimized by a fraudulent broker has no recourse against the person or entity that buys the security. Since each loan is spliced and becomes a part of many different securities, thousands of investors could be liable for the actions of a single broker if not for this doctrine.

Shortly after the Georgia fiasco, New Jersey went through a comparable experience. When the state passed a law that created similar liabilities for the secondary market, the agencies used the same tactic. This time the state dug in for a fight, and for a while it looked like the law would stick. But eventually the state gave in, realizing the fight couldn't be won.

The agencies sent a powerful message in Georgia and New Jersey: Any predatory lending legislation that addressed secondary market liability would face strong resistance. Since then more than 20 states have passed predatory lending laws and none of them had confrontations with the agencies because they bypassed the issue of liability altogether.

Although the agencies executed their playbook under the guise of protecting the secondary market, they had other motives. Had either the Georgia or New Jersey law gone into effect, fewer loans would have been securitized. This would have meant less revenue for the agencies. Understanding that the laws would impact their bottom line, the agencies simultaneously protected investors and their own financial interests by mounting a fight.

I don't advocate overturning the Holder in Due Course doctrine. Any legislation that creates liability for the secondary market will negatively impact the securitization market and hurt the consumer. The most effective ways to solve this problem are discussed in Chapter 7. Nonetheless, Friedman's comment on the agencies was dead-on. Any group that can shut down a state's mortgage market is a powerful force.

Who's Running the Show?

Collectively, the rating agencies and investment firms dictated how the subprime market operated. As Wall Street determined the type of loans that could be financed, the agencies rated the securities so investors would purchase the bonds. While many states passed laws to regulate nondepository lenders, most neglected to address underwriting standards and product guidelines.

With little government oversight, Wall Street and the agencies became the de facto regulators of the industry. The implications of this are enormous. Both parties, driven by profit and shielded from liability, dictated how the market would function. Not only was the fox guarding the hen house, he hired a contractor and built a separate wing so he could feast at his convenience.

Lenders wrote mortgages based on what the investment banks

could securitize and the agencies would rate. If the secondary market dictated what loans it would buy and some of the most powerful companies in the world rated them as investment grade, how is a lender negligent for writing them? This is how lenders try to claim deniability.

That isn't a tactic to absolve lenders from potential wrongdoing. On the contrary, there's plenty of blame that needs to be distributed and lenders deserve a share. But any solution to this crisis will only be effective if it addresses the deficiencies of Wall Street and the rating agencies.

Rating New Products

In some ways, the rating agencies present a contradiction. On one hand, they consistently rated securities with riskier mortgage products as investment grade. On the other hand, they claimed the newer loan products had no track record of performance, which gave them an excuse if their assessments were wrong. To say there's no basis to compare performance, however, is not true.

John Mauldin, author of the August 11, 2007, article, "Back to the 1998 Crisis, Subprime to Impact for a Long Time," pulled a listing of all subprime Residential Mortgage-Backed Securities in Bloomberg. He sorted those with the most loans over 60 days past due to see what they showed. While the two worst performers were from 2006, many of the 20 worst performing securities were from 2000, 2001, and 2003, long before underwriting standards were loosened. Mauldin also noted that some of the mortgages from 2001 performed relatively well. His argument was that anyone who did their homework understood that performance was all over the board.

The agencies have stated that their models relied on historical data and that there wasn't enough information on popular items like stated income loans or piggyback loans (when first and second lien mortgages are closed simultaneously to avoid or minimize down payment requirements). Again, I find this logic to be faulty. Subprime piggyback mortgages were prevalent in the market as early as 2000. My company began offering 100 percent stated income loans through Countrywide with credit scores down to 620 in 2003. That's four to six years worth of data on billions of dollars in subprime mortgages.

This indicates the agencies' models may be deficient in several ways. First, using Countrywide as an example, the guidelines for subprime stated income loans changed very little during the last four years. As time went by, however, a larger percentage of loans met this criterion. While the data existed to evaluate the performance of these loans, it's possible the models didn't account for the increased risk of having a higher percentage of riskier mortgages. Second, the models didn't factor in market risk. When property values are rising, distressed borrowers can sell or refinance to get financial relief. As values stabilize or decline, borrowers have fewer options, which results in higher delinquencies.

In a senior-subordinate structure, the lower tranches are designed to protect the top ones. By accurately predicting the bottom tier will only fail to a certain degree, the senior groups remain shielded from loss. When the assumptions are faulty and lower tiers start to fall, the upper tranches become vulnerable. Ultimately, the agencies rated too high a percentage of the securities as investment grade and not enough in the lower tranches. It's like building a 12-foot-tall dam to hold back 20 feet of water.

Slow to Respond

The agencies have stated they're not responsible for policing the performance of mortgage-backed securities. While they do review performance, they're notoriously slow to change the ratings, believing a loan pool should show a sustainable pattern of loss before a downgrade should be considered. This strategy also shields them from scrutiny when a rating is horribly inaccurate.

If the agencies downgrade a security shortly after it's issued, credibility suffers. Imagine that a new pool of subprime loans experienced a higher rate of default than expected and kept getting worse each month. How would it look if AAA-rated mortgage-backed securities were downgraded just months after being issued? It would shake the entire investment community to its core and prove the agencies are either incompetent or compromised. Responding slowly allows the agencies to mask the extent of their mistakes.

The strategy worked well until late 2006, when investors noticed how poorly the 2005 and 2006 subprime securities were performing. Not only didn't the agencies sound the alarm, the worst performing securities weren't downgraded until several months after most subprime lenders had gone out of business. On July 9, 2007, Moody's announced that it would place 184 tranches of 91 CDOs on review for possible downgrade. The next day they issued an unprecedented 451 downgrades for first and second lien residential mortgage-backed securities. Since then the agencies have issued a massive number of downgrades, long after the poor performance of the securities became known. It's clear that somebody was asleep at the wheel.

How Securitization Impacts the Borrower

The present record homeownership levels are a direct result of securitization. The aggressive mortgage offerings that helped higher-risk borrowers to finance a home existed because the loan could be sold on the secondary market and packaged into a security. For all the good securitization has done, the long-term fallout we're about to experience may outweigh the short-term gain.

Securitization not only allowed unqualified borrowers to secure financing, it imposed restrictions on distressed borrowers who needed relief. In the days when borrowers dealt directly with a local bank for every aspect of the mortgage, the relationship was flexible. Local banks could sit face-to-face with a distressed borrower to hammer out a solution. Since the relationship was localized, the bank had other reasons to act responsibly. When institutions develop a strong local brand, it only takes one disgruntled consumer to create a firestorm of bad publicity.

Today, distressed borrowers have few options. If a defaulting homeowner is treated poorly, who is he going to mount his publicity campaign against? The broker has no liability for the loan. The subprime lender is probably out of business. The mortgage has been spliced into a hundred pieces so the borrower doesn't know who owns it. Even if he did, the Holder in Due Course doctrine makes it difficult to pursue legal action. There may be a separate servicing company but, depending on the borrower's circumstances, a loan modification may be difficult. Since defaults have recently soared, it has become apparent that most servicing companies aren't properly staffed to handle the influx of distressed borrowers.

While servicers would prefer to keep borrowers in the house making payments, providing them with relief has to make sense. A loan modification is most effective when it assists borrowers who've had a temporary setback, such as being out of work for a few months. If a borrower can resume making timely payments, the servicer is more inclined to work with him. But when a borrower just can't afford the payment, there's no reason to modify the mortgage.

While trustees and servicers have some discretion to modify loans or create repayment plans, the process isn't straightforward. Depending on how the rules are written within the securitization agreement, modification plans can lead to disputes between servicers and investors. Kurt Eggert, professor of law at Chapman University School of Law, refers to it as "tranche warfare."

In his April 17, 2007, testimony to the Committee on Senate Banking, Housing and Urban Affairs Subcommittee on Securities,

Insurance and Investments, Eggert discussed how the securitization process works to the detriment of the distressed borrower.

> Restructuring the loan poses a substantial fiduciary dilemma to the trustee, because it would almost inevitably involve removing some part of a stream of income from one tranche and adding income to another tranche. This "tranche warfare" is a significant brake on the flexibility to restructure a loan . . . One tranche might hold the right to any principal repayments made during the first year, another to interest payments during that year, yet another to interest payments during the second year, and so on.

In other words, stealing from one tranche to pay another creates legal challenges. Since mortgage-backed securities are broken down into complex payment streams, any effort to modify a loan would likely benefit one tranche at the expense of another. When trustees are faced with making such a choice, they open themselves to claims they breached their fiduciary duty. In the end, it's often easier for servicers and trustees to avoid using any discretion as a way to sidestep these disputes. This helps to explain why, according to Moody's Investors Service, servicers adjusted only 1 percent of subprime mortgages that had rates reset during the first six months of 2007.

What the Future Holds

There is little doubt that the housing and mortgage markets are in for a bumpy ride. Although Chapter 7 discusses potential solutions, there are no quick fixes or easy answers. I'm concerned that Congress will either pass ineffective legislation or the courts will take matters into their own hands. In some cases, it's already starting to happen.

In October 2007, a colleague shared with me his recent experience. He worked for a firm that securitized subprime and nonagency mortgages and he participated in a meeting to discuss a lawsuit against his firm. What's interesting is how the Holder in Due Course Doctrine didn't apply because of the special circumstances of this case. Here's his story:

> The borrower originally took a five-year ARM back in 2002. Since the broker and lender were both out of business, she filed a lawsuit against my firm, the company that securitized her mortgage. She told the judge she didn't understand what would happen to the interest rate when the loan adjusted. Her original interest rate was 4 percent and had gone to 7 percent a few months earlier. Her husband had cancer so the loan had become a hardship.
>
> I walk into the judge's chambers with our attorney and the first thing the judge says is he understands both sides of the case. But he wants to know what we're going do to help this woman. He expected us to fix the problem and keep it out of his courtroom.
>
> There are a couple of interesting things about the loan. To start, the borrowers both had great credit and income when they qualified. She was an A borrower who got a fair deal. She was also an intelligent, working professional who signed numerous disclosures, just like every other borrower, explaining what it meant to have an ARM. This wasn't someone who got duped. She either didn't read the documents or was just looking for a way out. In the five years she had the mortgage, she never missed a payment. When her husband contracted cancer and stopped working, she couldn't pay her property taxes, which I think prompted her lawsuit.
>
> I didn't think she had a legitimate case against anyone. But the judge felt sorry for her and wanted us to fix it to keep it out of his courtroom. We decided it wasn't worth the bad press that would come from fighting a woman whose husband was battling cancer. By the time we paid the court costs, her attorney's fees, back taxes and permanently modified her loan

to a fixed rate of 6.5%, we spent $100,000 to fix a loan that we never made and appeared to be in no way fraudulent or deceptive.

Her whole argument amounted to "I didn't understand." When someone who wasn't manipulated and that probably knew better got this kind of treatment, it opened my eyes. It made me wonder what someone with a legitimate grievance could get.

Secondary Contributors: The Fed, Consumers, Retail Lenders, Homebuilders, and Realtors

The preceding chapters show that the collapse of the mortgage market was a direct result of several groups acting in a deceptive or fraudulent manner. It took brokers manipulating loans, lenders financing unqualified borrowers, investment banks securitizing risky mortgages, and rating agencies validating these securities as investment grade to unleash the perfect storm. In all likelihood the full impact from this collective effort won't be known for years to come.

However, there are still some pieces of this story that need to be told. We'll start by examining how the secondary participants—the Federal Reserve, borrowers, retail lenders, homebuilders, and realtors—contributed to the problem. We'll then review the specific events and trends that led to the explosive growth and eventual demise of the subprime industry.

Secondary Contributors: The Federal Reserve

There's a large contingent who believe that Alan Greenspan and the Federal Reserve were the primary contributors to the housing and mortgage debacle. For me, discussing the actions of the Fed is not unlike the conundrum Greenspan talked about in his now-famous 2005 speech. The monetary policy employed by the Fed is a main reason anyone involved with subprime mortgages, or any form of lending for that matter, prospered during the last six years. I discussed the subject with a colleague at an industry conference in 2005, and his comments still resonate with me. He said, "Greenspan's decision to lower rates changed my life." Since he made more money in the previous four years than during his entire business career, it's easy to understand why. He wasn't alone in his thinking. The Fed's decision to lower the federal funds rate created a windfall the mortgage industry may never see again.

I face two challenges in discussing the role of the Fed. First, to accuse Greenspan of poor judgment would be hypocritical. The financial gains my company achieved were a by-product of the Fed's actions. To call him negligent, knowing that I cheered every time new rate cuts were announced, comes across as disingenuous. Second, I understand the basic workings of the Fed but economic policy is not my forte. I've read volumes on the subject, books written by some of the smartest economists and policy makers in the country. While many view his tenure at the Fed as nothing short of genius, there are some, like Alan Abelson of *Barron's*, who take a contrary position. His article in the August 13, 2007, issue of that magazine summarizes the perspective that is closest to my own:

> As we watched the great unraveling of that tangled web that financial engineering spun, we couldn't help but think of the acute discomfort being felt by that outstanding public servant Alan Greenspan, who, during his celebrated tenure as head of the Federal Reserve, more than anyone deserves credit for nurturing the ownership society. Mr. Greenspan, lest we for-

get, went far beyond the call to entice people, no matter what their circumstances, into buying a home by whacking the cost of credit to as near zero as you can get and still lay claim to being somewhat rational, and urging them to go for those new-fangled adjustable mortgages with deceptively low initial interest rates.

Beyond even his cleverness at blowing successive "smart bubbles," so that the newest one (for example, housing) was nicely calculated to offset the fallout from its burst predecessor (the stock market), and his adroit ability to please his political masters . . .

Financial mischief on such a grand scale is not a one-man job, and Mr. Greenspan, needless to say, had a lot of help from Wall Street, Washington, and points north, south, and west. But there's no diminishing the singular part he played.

And just as the contempt for risk that made possible the gross extravagances in housing and the financial markets was sustained by confidence that Mr. G would always bail out the participants—the so-called Greenspan put—so the current collapse in housing and the financial markets merits a special designation, one that similarly recognizes his critical role. How about the Greenspan Kaput?

What I find to be most telling about Greenspan's tenure is how he, by his own admission, misunderstood what was happening in the subprime market. In 2004 he went so far as to praise the industry for safely extending access to credit for people once excluded from the housing market. Ironically, his comments occurred about the same time we started to question whether the subprime business model made sense given the cracks showing in the system.

Borrowers

Let's be honest. As consumers, we couldn't help ourselves. As if the temptation to max out our credit cards wasn't bad enough, the lure of cheap money was impossible to resist. Whether it meant buying a bigger home, refinancing to a lower interest rate, or tapping into home equity, this was a once in a lifetime opportunity.

Unfortunately, when opportunity comes knocking, greed and ignorance are not far behind. The following examples represent the kind of loan applications we underwrote on a daily basis. They show how a wide range of borrowers, even those not manipulated by brokers or lenders, contributed to the demise of the industry. To do them justice, I've adapted comedian Jeff Foxworthy's classic routine *You Might Be A Redneck If . . .* to the mortgage industry.

- If you ever signed a federal home loan application knowing your income wasn't reported correctly . . . You may have set yourself up for mortgage disaster.

- If you viewed your home as an ATM machine and continued to cash out time and again . . . You may have set yourself up for mortgage disaster.

- If you flipped spec properties with regularity and you're now stuck with deals you can't unload . . . You *are* headed for mortgage disaster.

- If you took out an ARM loan because the ultralow teaser rate was the only way you could qualify . . . You *did* set yourself up for mortgage disaster (unless the government says you qualify for a rate freeze).

And finally . . .

- If you signed a promissory note and thought the line "I promise to pay" was more of an option than a requirement . . . *You are truly a subprime borrower.*

All kidding aside, there's nothing humorous about the fact that nearly two million people might lose their homes to foreclosure in the next few years. However, I have no sympathy for borrowers who knew what they were doing but still blame mortgage lenders for their problems. Cheap money and easy credit may be hard to resist, but that doesn't justify letting greed and ignorance drive your decisionmaking.

What percentage of borrowers currently in default (at least 30 days late) fit this description? The answer is speculative, but my conservative estimate is that at least half of all borrowers understood what they were getting into, probably more. Still, to say 50 percent of borrowers didn't understand what they were doing raises another concern. Is it possible the majority of consumers entered into the largest financial decision of their lives despite being unaware of what they had gotten themselves into?

The government, for all its efforts in this area, has done more to create confusion than to protect the consumer. When a loan closes, borrowers sign enough documents to make their head spin. I've had seven mortgages in my life, and every time I walked out of the loan closing I wondered why the process had to be so complicated. For the first-time homebuyer, the process is often overwhelming. On many occasions I've seen borrowers at the closing table develop that deer in the headlights look.

Though the process is far too confusing, each document does provide the borrower with some vital piece of information. There may be a lot of paperwork to understand, but ignorance is not a valid excuse. To protect themselves at closing, borrowers should get the answers to five questions:

1. What is the payment and can you afford it? Be certain to ask whether this includes the property taxes and insurance.
2. Is this the correct type of mortgage? In other words, is it a fixed-rate or an adjustable-rate mortgage? If it's an ARM, is it clear to you how and when the rate will adjust?
3. Is the loan amount correct?
4. Is there a prepayment penalty? If so, do you understand what it means and how it will work?

5. Do the closing costs closely resemble the figures provided on the Good Faith Estimate? The loan officer should explain in detail any variation greater than 1/2 percent of the loan amount.

Getting the answer to these questions helps the borrower to be sure that the loan is correct. The potential for confusion arises from having to sign dozens of documents, with no time to read them, when a one-page form would do the trick. As this book was going to press, Congress was considering whether such a document should be used for all mortgages. In my opinion, that would go a long way toward simplifying the process.

Income and Down Payment Become Optional

While ultralow interest rates started the boom, aggressive under-writing standards kept the wheels turning even as rates started to rise. The numbers from my company, which are indicative of what took place within the industry as a whole, tell an interesting story. In 2001, stated income loans represented 25 percent of our busi-ness, while 15 percent of borrowers financed with no money down (or no equity in the case of a refinance). By 2004, the figures rose to 35 and 38 percent, respectively. By 2006, just over 50 percent of borrowers financed with no money down even as property values were starting to retreat.

Let's put this in perspective. As early as 2004, only one out of four borrowers was financing a home using a down payment *and* proving income. I doubt that the industry's founders could have foreseen a day when the fundamental principles of risk manage-ment would no longer apply. Did the broker steer consumers toward these loans? No question. Were lenders writing loans that never should have been written? Absolutely. Throw in the actions of Wall Street and the rating agencies and you've got one heck of a mess. But to stop there is shortsighted. When a borrower signs on the dotted line, he must be held accountable.

I'll jump on my soapbox for a moment. If borrowers had been slightly more responsible, this crisis wouldn't be as severe. Having been taught to never borrow more than I can afford to pay, their actions strike me as reckless, which may sound peculiar coming from a former subprime lender. Admittedly, mortgaging my parents' home to fund my company makes preaching fiscal responsibility seem a bit hypocritical, but there's a big difference between taking a well-timed and calculated risk and putting yourself into a position where you are highly likely to default on a loan.

In a country where the government can't balance its own checkbook, consumers live on credit, and the collective savings rate is zero, we've become conditioned to spend first and figure out how to pay for it later. The allure of cheap money and easy credit was too much to resist, especially for those borrowers who could least afford it.

Retail Mortgage Lenders

I've avoided discussing direct lenders until now for several reasons. First, brokers originated the majority of all subprime mortgages, which meant they were the primary drivers of the product. Second, most subprime loans originated by retail lenders were done through big companies, lenders like Countrywide and Wells Fargo. Having worked on the wholesale side of the business, my experience is best suited to discussing this business channel.

However, a book on subprime lending wouldn't be complete without mentioning Ameriquest Mortgage. In my opinion, this lender did more to give subprime lending a bad name than any other company. In January 2006 Ameriquest settled a lawsuit with state prosecutors and lending regulators for $325 million, resolving allegations that the company defrauded and misled consumers. While their tactics are now well documented, it wasn't until we hired two former Ameriquest employees that I learned what these tactics were. Our new employees told us that at Ameriquest every loan was supposed to charge the maximum fees, interest rates, and prepayment penalties in order to make the company money. The business model focused heavily on cash-out mortgages, which enabled Ameriquest to collect front-end fees from the borrower's equity. The "stick it to the consumer" mentality they described to me translated into borrowers being charged, on average, three to four points in loan origination fees. If you want more information on the company's tactics, just Google "Ameriquest Mortgage." There are numerous blogs that include stories from disgruntled customers.

The greatest irony comes in the aftermath of the settlement. It's widely believed that Roland Arnall, billionaire founder of the company and a major contributor to George W. Bush's campaign, agreed to the settlement to clear the way for his confirmation vote in the U.S. Senate. Exactly 20 days after the settlement was announced, Mr. Arnall received Senate approval as the U.S. Ambassador to the Netherlands. I wonder if presidential candidate Barack Obama, who wants to prosecute all negligent subprime lenders, would have included Mr. Arnall if he made it to the White House. As it turns out we'll never know. Mr. Arnall died in Spring 2008.

In the meantime, I've written President Bush asking for the next ambassador position that comes available. Since Mr. Arnall and I both ran subprime mortgage companies, and I didn't have to pay one-third of a billion dollars as a result of my business practices, it stands to reason that I'm well suited for the job. Of course, not having contributed millions to the Bush campaign might explain why I'm still waiting for a response.

Homebuilders and Realtors

If mortgage brokers helped steer the subprime industry off a cliff, homebuilders and realtors were only too happy to come along for the ride. I've combined these categories for the purposes of our discussion and left them for last because their actions had a minor impact compared to the other players.

After leaving my company, I worked for TBI Mortgage, the builder-owned mortgage company of Toll Brothers Inc., a luxury homebuilder. Builder-owned mortgage companies exist primarily to help the builder sell more homes. Profitability and controlling the loan are important, but home sales generate far more income than mortgage loans. Since no other type of lender has selling homes as a primary objective, builder-owned mortgage companies are an anomaly. Serving two masters, borrower and builder, can also put them in a difficult position. One experience during my tenure at TBI showed how contentious this relationship can get.

A customer in Raleigh, North Carolina, was buying a model townhome in a golf course community, which meant it came fully furnished. The purchase price was $452,000 but there was a problem with the appraisal. Like every other townhome in the community, the value came in at $400,000, more than $50,000 below the contract price. The furniture was worth another $15,000, but mortgage guidelines don't allow it to be included in a home's value. This created a problem on several fronts. First, the builder was upset that we didn't get an appraised value to support the purchase price. Does this sound familiar? As the VP of sales for the region, I usually didn't get involved in specific loan files unless there was a problem. It took me some time to make the builder realize why we couldn't provide an overvalued appraisal. Second, when the buyer found out about the appraised value he naturally became upset. Asking someone to pay $50,000 over market value has that effect on people.

The builder eventually lowered the price and the buyer brought in more cash to make the deal work. Shortly before the loan closed, I discovered the builder had ordered an appraisal when construction started months earlier. Do you want to guess the value his appraiser came with up? It was $400,000. The builder knew the home wasn't worth $450,000, didn't notify the mortgage company that he already had the property appraised, and still expected us to close it at the inflated value.

This story isn't meant to paint Toll Brothers in a negative light. In general, aside from the tough business culture, they were a well-run organization. The example shows that builders, like everyone else, were focused on driving profits, even if it meant sticking it to the buyer.

In many ways, real estate agents resemble mortgage brokers. They only make money if the deal closes, and while they can represent the buyer or the seller, in most states they can also represent both parties at once. The independent nature of their business can lead to abusive behavior.

My friend Rich Trombetta, business owner and author of *Mustard Doesn't Go on Corn*, shares his experiences with Realtors.

> My wife and I were going to open houses on a Sunday when we came across a great house that we loved and wanted to make an offer. We spoke to the Realtor hosting the open house and he gave us his cell phone and contact information and asked us to call that evening. Although we were looking at homes we were not using a Realtor to assist with our search.
>
> That night we made an offer and we were in back and forth contact with the Realtor from the open house. What happened next absolutely floored me. He told us our offer was slightly less than another offer that had come in that day but he would rather work with us since he would get the entire commission for the sale. Otherwise, he would have to split the commission with another Realtor who was representing the people that made the second offer.
>
> I asked him, "Let me make sure I understand this. You would rather present a lower offer to your clients so that you receive a higher commission?" He was silent. I told him, "I don't like this. I am not sure if I should contact the sellers, the attorney general, or your office manager." He started to get defensive and I simply said good-bye and hung up the phone.
>
> I have never trusted a Realtor since.

Of course there are plenty of Realtors that do an excellent job for their clients but, depending on whom we believe, the data paint some different conclusions. The National Association of Realtors (NAR) claims that the average seller who uses a real estate professional makes 16 percent more on the sale of a home than do sellers who go it alone. Although there's no data to support this claim, it seems plausible that using a professional to sell any product will net a higher price than selling on your own.

Steven Levitt and Stephen Dubner, authors of *Freakonomics: A Rogue Economist Explores the Hidden Side of Everything*, share a different view. They obtained home-sale data from the Chicago area and discovered that realtor-owned homes stayed on the market 10 percent longer and made 3 to 4 percent more than homes sold for nonrealtors. They showed that economics is the study of incentives—how people get what they need, especially when others want the same thing. In the case of realtors, they believe that when an agent sells his own home, the incentive to hold out for an additional $10,000, for example, is great. As the homeowner, the realtor gets to keep the entire amount. When the same situation is applied to selling a client's home, the realtor stands to gain only an additional $600 (based on a 6 percent commission). The relative payoff is so small that it isn't worth marketing the property for a longer period.

Levitt and Dubner write in Chapter 4 of their book:

> We smirk now when we think of ancient cultures that embraced faulty causes—the warriors who believed, for instance that it was their raping of a virgin that brought them victory on the battlefield. But we too embrace faulty causes, usually at the urging of an ancient expert proclaiming a truth in which he has a vested interest.

The Demise of the Industry

As early as eight years ago, a series of events and trends began that promoted the rapid growth and contributed to the eventual decline of subprime lending. I've broken them down as follows:

- Three industry-specific events that helped subprime lending to expand.

- What happened when lenders experienced lapses in judgment.
- The decline in profitability.
- How new and incompetent brokers impacted the industry.
- The development of new and riskier mortgage products.

The Keys to Growth

Beginning in 2000, several events occurred that promoted the expansion of subprime lending. While each one was independently significant, the collective impact served as a major catalyst for growth.

First, Standard and Poor's (S&P) concluded the piggyback mortgage (where the customer took out a simultaneous second loan in lieu of a down payment) was no more likely to default than a single loan. The other agencies took the same position shortly thereafter. While the event went largely unnoticed outside of the industry, its impact was important.

Bill Dallas, viewed by many as a mortgage innovator, was the first to offer a 100 percent mortgage in partnership with Freddie Mac. He also believed the piggyback, or 80-20 mortgage, would perform as well as the single 100 percent loan provided the FICO score was over 680. By adopting a more liberal set of credit standards, the rating agencies effectively gave birth to the subprime piggyback mortgage. Within a few years, this product became an industry staple.

It wasn't until six years later that S&P reversed its decision, determining that piggybacks had a much higher probability of default. Their initial decision proved disastrous. In July 2007, Moody's made the unprecedented move to downgrade every second-lien securitization it had rated from 2005 to the present. It's clear the rating agencies' initial announcement had been based on faulty assumptions.

Second, the decision on piggybacks also affected the mortgage insurance (MI) industry. MI companies provide coverage to lenders for loans over 80 percent loan-to-value (LTV) in case of borrower default. Since the ruling allowed second-lien mortgages to be used in place of mortgage insurance, the decision effectively neutered the MI industry and created a void.

Before S&P's announcement, a lender that wanted to offer a loan product over 80 percent LTV required MI to securitize the product. Since profitability was tied to effective risk management, most MI companies would err on the side of caution. They performed a check-and-balance function, which kept the industry thinking rationally and restricted lenders from implementing products that were poorly conceived.

Third, the GSEs (government-sponsored enterprises)—Fannie Mae and Freddie Mac—experienced their own problems a few years later. A deep look into their accounting practices revealed that, unlike other business scandals in which companies tried to hide losses, the GSEs made so much profit they were attempting to spread their income out over time.

Once their accounting practices became headline news, auditors were brought in to sort things out. That fact that the GSEs tried to alter their financials was enough incentive for Congress to impose restrictions. The decision to place caps on their portfolios ultimately hindered their ability to grow. At a time when the industry was experiencing record volume, the GSEs were made to sit in the penalty box. If they hadn't been restricted, the GSEs could have played a more active role in the secondary market.

The combination of all three events—the growth of piggyback mortgages, the neutralization of the MI companies, and the punishment of the GSEs—removed the last barriers to growth for the subprime industry. With the investment banks and rating agencies left to serve as the industry's moral compass, effective risk management gave way to reckless behavior.

Lapses in Judgment

Lapses in judgment are nothing new in the industry. Occasionally a subprime lender was too aggressive with a product offering, thinking they'd found an ingenious way to recreate the risk model. Inevitably, the product performed poorly and at Kellner we'd attribute the lender's action to temporary insanity.

After the first subprime meltdown in 1997, The Associates (purchased by Citigroup in 2000) offered a 95 percent loan-to-value program (5 percent down payment) for borrowers with 540 credit scores. Historically, the product required a minimum credit score of 560 to 580, since default models indicated loan performance dropped precipitously below that level. Their decision to break from conventional thinking reminded me of the Roadrunner cartoons, with The Associates playing the part of Wile E. Coyote, super genius.

When The Associates paid us 600 basis points for using the product, we thought someone in their trading department had spiked the water cooler. As a new company struggling to survive, we were happy to use this product and it was instrumental in helping us to get over the initial hump. In our first four months, it represented nearly 40 percent of our business. It had the two things every subprime wholesale lender wanted—a unique niche and a high margin. Given the absurdity of the product, it seemed only fitting that the first mortgage we ever closed, which fit its guideline, went to foreclosure less than a year later. There was nothing fraudulent or deceptive about the deal. It was just a high-risk loan based on a flawed risk model.

The product offering was short lived. When Citigroup purchased The Associates, they immediately discontinued the program. Some time later, a colleague confirmed what many of us had already expected—the product performed poorly.

Another profound lapse in judgment occurred in 2003 when RFC offered 100 percent financing for borrowers with 560 credit scores. Until that point, it was generally accepted that 580 was the minimum score. Writing a 100 percent loan with a 560 score was like swimming with sharks—it was only a matter of time until you were bitten.

At Kellner we viewed RFC's program as a desperate act. Always the conservative stalwart, RFC seldom pushed the risk envelope. When I worked for them in 1998, one of their more unusual product offerings was a 125 percent loan, which was a second-lien mortgage that allowed consumers to borrow up to 125 percent of the value of their homes. When this industry segment imploded, RFC was the only major investor left standing. They built a reputation as a smart and conservative company because they understood how to manage risk.

When the Wall Street investment banks started capturing a larger share of the subprime market, RFC quickly fell behind. In a few years they went from being a top five investor to barely making the top 20. The 100 percent product was intended to help them reclaim market share.

Offered only to select customers, the product proved to be a disaster. Seldom in the history of mortgage lending had a new product been so quickly pulled from the market. It showed how the pressure to compete for market share could wear down even the smartest lenders.

This should have sounded some alarm bells. If a company widely regarded as the leader in managing risk for nonagency mortgages experienced such a profound lapse in judgment, how would other, less-skilled investors respond to the pressure?

Profit Margins

From 2000 to 2002 we were paid between 450 to 500 basis points (bps) for each loan sold. In some cases the figure exceeded 500 bps, as evidenced by The Associates example, but that was the exception. By 2003 we started experiencing a marked decline in profitability. With over 100 subprime wholesale mortgage companies competing for business, lenders grew volume at the expense of profit margin.

Table 6.1 shows what happened to our profits from 2003 through 2005. The numbers are strictly for illustration purposes and don't represent actual revenue. The first year serves as a baseline with 100 loans equaling $100 in revenue. This chart shows how the following years stacked up relative to 2003. It doesn't take a Wharton graduate to realize the business model was headed for disaster. Although volume was growing, net revenue per loan was dropping

Table 6.1 Net Revenue Comparisons

	Number of Loans	Total Revenue	Revenue per Loan
2003	100	$100	$1.00
2004	145	$75	$0.55
2005	210	$50	$0.30

fast. Even though expenses increased as result of growing the business, the decline was largely a result of being paid less for the product. Conversations with our competitors indicated they were experiencing a similar trend.

Several things contributed to this decline. First, the largest subprime lenders started a price war. Companies like New Century and Argent offered rates that weren't compatible with the risk levels. We tried to win customers by offering stellar service and for a while it worked. But once technology leveled the playing field, our competitors improved their service. We had to shrink our profit margins to remain competitive.

The pricing pressures meant small and medium-sized lenders were hit the hardest. The same investors who purchased our loans had wholesale divisions that undercut our pricing. Since the biggest lenders put loans directly into a security, their margins were higher, which enabled them to compete better in a price war. As a pass-through lender, another layer in the food chain, we didn't have that luxury.

Second, it's no coincidence our revenue peaked just as the fed funds rate bottomed out. While that indicator doesn't dictate fixed mortgage rates, it influences the overall cost of money, which impacts interest rates for ARMs. Keep in mind that most subprime loans are adjustable rate, not fixed. Kellner's ARM to fixed product ratio was 80/20, similar to most of our competitors. As the Fed increased the funds rate by more than 4 percent from 2004 to 2006, interest rates for subprime ARMs remained flat. The only way for revenues to keep pace was to increase loan production.

Watching this scenario unfold, I realized the industry was losing touch with reality. I frequently spoke with a colleague and competitor who owned Concorde Acceptance Corporation and we would talk about the state of the industry. We often discussed the risk-reward curve, which helped analyze the effectiveness of our business model. By late 2004 we both felt the business had reached a point where the risk of being a wholesale subprime lender outweighed the financial rewards.

Rational thinking dictates that when the cost of money goes up, interest rates should follow. While some reduction in margin is acceptable and expected in a highly competitive market, the leading subprime companies took it to the extreme. Unfortunately, as margins were getting squeezed, the most critical factor was being ignored—risk.

At a basic level, mortgage lending is nothing more than effective risk management. If a lender offers a high-risk product and profit margins continue to drop, one of two things must happen. The lender either increases interest rates or tightens underwriting guidelines to compensate for the reduced margin and subsequent risk. Not only did the industry choose to ignore both principles, it went in the opposite direction by developing more aggressive products.

New Products—A Meltdown of Epic Proportions

If the subprime industry was teetering on the edge of a cliff, relaxed underwriting standards pushed it over the edge. Before discussing the particulars, here is a quick recap of the events leading to the industry's demise.

- With the advent of the piggyback mortgage and the neutralization of mortgage insurance companies and government-sponsored enterprises, investment firms and rating agencies were left to regulate the industry.
- Interest rates fell to record lows, creating a frenzy among consumers to acquire investment properties, treat their homes like

ATM machines, or achieve the American dream by owning a home regardless of whether they could afford it.

- By 2003 brokers were originating the majority of all subprime loans. By 2006, the figure peaked at 63 percent. With many loan officers new to the business, this unregulated and unsupervised group of originators took a bad situation and made it worse.

- The intense pricing war among subprime lenders caused a reduction in profit margins. For revenues to keep pace required lenders to finance more borrowers, which led to the development of less restrictive underwriting standards.

- Since the agencies were overly aggressive in how they rated subprime securities, the stage was set for riskier loan products to enter the mix.

There are enough examples of foolish product offerings and guideline changes to fill an entire chapter. I've detailed a few of them to provide some insight on how the industry lost its sensibilities. Looking back, it's clear that each was a disaster waiting to happen.

- **100 Percent Stated Income Loan.** Even though Countrywide wasn't the only lender to offer stated income loans, their offering was risky. Lending to borrowers with no down payment and no proof of income had merit as long as their credit scores were high (700+). Countrywide offered this product to self-employed borrowers with 620 scores and wage earners with 640 scores.

  When stated income loans were developed in the 1980s, they were designed specifically for the self-employed borrower. They required a sizable down payment, excellent credit history, and intense scrutiny of the appraisal. Allowing a borrower who earned a set wage to qualify for this program was not an option. But once borrowers with mediocre credit could finance with no down payment and no income verification, it was the beginning of the end. Since the interest rate was only slightly higher for stated income loans compared to full income documentation, brokers opted for the path of least resistance. Was there any need to bother with collecting tax returns and pay stubs when the interest rate for a stated income loan was only three-eighths of a percent higher?

- **Investment Property Loans.** While low interest rates fueled the market for investment properties, riskier mortgage products took the demand to another level. A subprime product that historically required a minimum down payment of 10 percent and proof of income was being offered with no money down and no income verification. At one point, lenders advertised the loan for borrowers with 660 credit scores, enabling speculators to simultaneously purchase multiple properties. As a result, speculative buying in markets like Las Vegas and Miami artificially inflated property values to unsustainable levels.

- **Guideline Changes.** While credit score was an excellent indicator of loan performance, its reliability was predicated on holding other credit factors (housing history, bankruptcies, and so on) constant. This was another area where logic failed. For example, by no longer requiring solid rental verification (allowing private verifications in its place), the risk models were skewed even further. When borrowers with bad credit, no money, no verifiable income, and no history of paying rent were approved for mortgages, why would anyone be surprised that the loans defaulted?

  The only product Wall Street didn't create was a stated credit loan. Could you imagine the conversation? So Mr. Johnson, what's your credit score? What's that you say, 750? Congratulations, you're approved!

- **A Classic Screw-Up.** As the implosion of 2007 drew near, HSBC (previously Household Finance), the company that led the industry for years in 100 percent financing with 580 credit scores, suffered a psychotic break. For nearly a decade, this product had *always* required a 12-month housing history of no more than one 30-day late payment. When HSBC announced that borrowers with 580 scores and a 90-day late payment for housing history could qualify for 100 percent financing, it was clear that someone in the risk department had lost his mind. It didn't matter if a borrower was one step away from foreclosure, HSBC would finance the purchase of a new home with no down payment. Even though that product lasted only a few months, it still ranks as one of the worst offerings in the history of subprime lending.

The Walls Come Down

As the 2006 subprime book of business started showing abysmal levels of performance, investors conducted a mass exodus from the secondary market. With no appetite for the product, the subprime industry experienced a total meltdown. One person started a web site, www.lenderimplode.com, to keep track of companies that went out of business or filed bankruptcy. He referred to the list as the lender implode-o-meter. In the first five months of 2007, more than 80 lenders (or divisions of companies) had shut down or gone out of business. By April 2008, the list topped 250.

In perhaps the cruelest of ironies, the fallout from subprime carried over a few months later to the prime side. With the investment community retreating from all nonagency mortgage-backed securities, the Alt-A market collapsed as well. Conservative lenders that never originated a subprime mortgage were left with no buyers for their products, so even they started going out of business.

Like dozens of other lenders, Kellner closed its doors in spring 2007—#44 on the implode-o-meter. Though Ken Orman was adept at staying ahead of the curve, even he couldn't envision just how bad things would get. With no investors willing to pay a premium for our product, he had no alternative but to shut down the company.

Having left 16 months earlier, I managed to bypass most of the destruction. I never could have imagined that my house catching fire would be a blessing in disguise, but that's how I've come to view the experience. Although Mike Elliott, our third partner, also left months earlier, Ken managed to find a few outlets to sell his remaining loans and walked away relatively unscathed. Selling them on the scratch and dent market was an expensive proposition, but nothing compared to the losses suffered by lenders who stuck it out a little longer.

As attorneys and politicians spend months, possibly years, trying to sort out this mess, there are some pressing questions still to address. At the top of the list is whether anything can be done to minimize the damage. Certainly there are no easy answers. The next and final chapter of this book addresses the current crisis and discusses some of the solutions under consideration. It is crucially important that all of us consider the future of the industry and the systemic changes that need to be implemented.

CHAPTER 7

How to Fix a Broken Industry

If the first six chapters have accomplished nothing else, they've shown that the subprime problems are multidimensional. From the brokers to the rating agencies, every player shares responsibility for this crisis. Since the issues we're currently facing are the result of a collective effort, the solution must be comprehensive as well. Unless the fundamental flaws that exist at every level of the mortgage food chain are properly addressed, any effort to change the way the industry operates will fall short. I've exposed the inner workings of the subprime industry in the hope that this information can serve as a guide to changing policy.

The key to effective legislation is striking a balance by protecting the consumer from predatory behavior while not restricting the availability of credit to borrowers who present a good risk. The question is whether Congress can solve the problem without going too far. While borrowers in the near term will face reduced mortgage options regardless of how the legislature responds, my concern is for the longterm.

We'll eventually work our way through this crisis. There will be a lot of pain and finger-pointing along the way, but a time will come when subprime mortgage financing, in some form, makes its way back into the marketplace. Why do I believe this? Because at the very heart of subprime lending, beneath the greed and the ineptitude that overtook the industry, is a business model that can provide value to the homebuyer.

After closing thousands of loans for subprime borrowers who made timely payments, I understand subprime's capabilities, good and bad. While the upside is likely to be overlooked in light of the current housing crisis, I know the positives can far outweigh the negatives, provided the business stays grounded in the basic principles of risk management. My objective is to show that a middle ground is possible—one that protects the consumer and still allows the market to determine what constitutes an acceptable credit risk.

Since the topic is a high priority among politicians, it's possible that a national predatory lending law will be in place by the time you read this book. The House of Representatives passed a predatory lending bill and the Senate is expected to do the same in 2008. As I explain my plan to address each of the industry players and develop lending standards to protect consumers, I'll use the House bill for comparison.

A Plan for Change

If there's one word that best describes my proposed solutions, it's accountability. Industry players who acted in a fraudulent or deceptive manner did so because there were few consequences for their actions. Although it's not feasible for every player in the food chain to be held responsible, there are ways to discourage or reduce predatory behavior.

Let's begin with the investment banks and rating agencies that handle the securities and the brokers who originate the loans. If you're wondering why I don't include lenders, it's because there's no need to discuss them separately as long as we address the issues at both ends of the mortgage process and develop lending standards that all mortgage companies must adhere to.

Investment Banks—Creating Liability

The idea of holding investment banks that securitize mortgages accountable for their actions has promise. It goes against the Holder in Due Course doctrine, but a limited form of assignee liability that targets securitizers is conceivable, provided it doesn't extend to the investors who purchase the bonds. Any effort to extend liability to bondholders would mean the end of mortgage securitization as we know it. But if borrowers have recourse against securitizers, it creates accountability. It's difficult to hide behind a veil of deception when there's an underlying threat of litigation.

The predatory lending bill passed in the House of Representatives creates limited assignee liability by defining the parameters of a "qualified" mortgage. If a loan doesn't meet a long list of guidelines and it's placed into a mortgage-backed security, the securitizer could be held liable. However, there are two concerns. First, the proposal faces an uphill battle in the Senate. Given the current climate in Washington, this provision will probably need to be removed in order for the legislation to pass, so the issue of assignee liability may become a moot point. Second, by creating boundaries for what is and is not a qualified mortgage, the bill restricts the availability of credit to the consumer.

The credit restrictions would apply primarily in two areas. First, they would severely restrict the use of most stated income loans. Although many people support the elimination of this product in light of how it was abused, I still believe that kind of loan makes sense under the right conditions. This product will be addressed later in this chapter. Second, the bill would create an annual percentage rate (APR) cap of 1.75 percent above the market rate for a 30-year conforming mortgage. Unlike the interest rate, APR represents the total cost of credit to the consumer, which takes into account one-time fees like loan origination and processing. Although interest rate and APR are not the same, they are often close in range when the fees being charged are not excessive. Therefore, you can view the 1.75 percent above market figure as an interest rate cap to keep things simple.

While the idea of mandating a rate cap might appear to be good for the consumer, it has the opposite effect. This provision would prevent borrowers who are a B credit grade or lower from obtaining a mortgage, and this group represents 15 to 20 percent of all subprime borrowers. If you believe these borrowers pose too great of a risk, consider the bigger picture. Anyone classified as a B grade or lower must provide a minimum down payment of 15 percent. They are a higher risk, but these borrowers aren't the reason we're in our current predicament. The problem was largely a function of lending money to borrowers at higher credit grades with no money down and no proof of income. Borrowers in the B grade category never had that option. Although I don't support a plan that restricts credit, an alternative solution is to move the APR cap another 100 basis points, to a total of 2.75 percent. That should allow the majority of borrowers to obtain financing.

If the Senate doesn't allow assignee liability to be included, there's another alternative that would require some effort on the part of the mortgage industry. Chapter 2 showed a credit matrix from RFC, explaining how borrowers are assigned grades based on their credit profile. Each lender developed an independent matrix, which meant the industry had no uniform standard. Expanding on the idea of credit grades to develop an industry-wide classification system for all mortgages could make the securitization process more transparent. John Mauldin initially suggested the idea in his weekly commentary "Outside the Box."

Here is how the idea works. The industry would develop multiple standards. One standard (class AAA for example) might include loans with a maximum loan-to-value (LTV) of 75 percent, debt-to-income (DTI) ratios of 25 percent, FICO scores of 740+, and so on.

Another standard (class AA) would have maximum LTVs of 80 percent, DTI ratios of 30 percent, and scores of 720+. These standards would apply to all companies that create mortgages.

When an investment bank packages a mortgage-backed security made up of thousands of loans, it could develop a class AAA standard security. With very clear payment and default risks, the agencies could give ratings based on these standards. By assigning every mortgage a classification, loans would be identified by their risk characteristics. With every loan class representing a different level of risk, investors could determine how much exposure they're willing to take. If there is a market for subprime loans, it would redevelop over time.

Implementation would require the cooperation of mortgage industry leaders, investment banks, and rating agencies. Even though all three parties have a vested interest in restoring order to the industry, the process would still be challenging since reaching a consensus would not be easy. However, developing a standard for all mortgage products could have a significant impact. At the very least, it would take some of the mystery out of the securitization process.

The Rating Agencies—A Major Overhaul

In late 2006, Congress passed the Credit Agency Reform Act requiring agencies to register with the Securities and Exchange Commission (SEC). Granting the SEC oversight has also given them enforcement capability. Time will tell whether the SEC does anything of substance with this authority, but there are some positive signs. They've already signaled that the agencies must disclose their procedures and methodologies for assigning ratings, which is a step in the right direction.

New authority aside, there are several ways to remedy the inherent flaws within this system. First, a separation of the advisory and rating functions should be mandated. The conflict of interest that arises from helping to structure securities and then rate them has already been discussed.

Second, the agencies should be required to regularly review and rerate debt securities. Even though this function is currently performed, there are no standards. Developing a systematic process for monitoring performance and adjusting the ratings would make the agencies more accountable. Had this been in place in 2005, it's conceivable that the downgrades would have sounded the alarm bells much earlier. There's also a third option. It would be difficult to implement and more radical in approach, but it would fix the problem.

For three years I paid a man to hang Christmas lights on my house. His price was so reasonable that most of my neighbors used him as well. As soon as Thanksgiving was over, he'd hang the lights, get paid, and take them down after the holidays. Since he proved trustworthy, none of us had an issue with paying him the entire fee once he hung the lights. On the third year he disconnected his phone shortly after Christmas, ending his reign as our favorite Christmas light guy. Since he already had our money, there was no motivation to finish the work.

Most of us are paid with the understanding that we'll produce a certain quality of work. Poor performance usually means losing a job. The agencies, however, operate under a different set of rules. They're paid the same regardless of performance and there's no motivation to replace them unless they are too conservative in their efforts. If ratings are judgments on whether a bond will pay interest on schedule until it matures, why aren't the agencies compensated against this measurement? The only way to change the agencies' behavior is to change their motivation.

The solution is to defer a portion of the agencies' income and tie it to the accuracy of their work. This isn't designed to pay the agencies less money, just to link income to performance. Under this scenario a portion of the fees paid to the agencies by investment banks, say 30 percent, is put into an escrow account for 12 or 18 months. Let's assume a security is expected to produce a specific return based on the rating. If the security performs as projected, the agencies receive the full amount of the deferred income. If the security performs worse than expected, the agency receives less.

An agency could provide an overly conservative rating to maximize the deferred income, but the natural forces of the market would likely prevent this from taking place since investment banks want the agencies to be aggressive.

What happens to the deferred income that doesn't get paid to the agencies? The same way mortgage insurance protects a lender in cases of default, the excess funds could compensate investors in cases of substantial loss. At the very least, it could restore confidence in the MBS market. Another option would be to use the funds to support a housing-related charity like Habitat for Humanity.

Under this system the agencies are motivated to monitor a security's performance and to be accurate with the initial rating. Of course, the SEC would have to work with the agencies to define expected default rates for each type of security, but that shouldn't be a difficult task given the available data. Once in place, the standards would serve as a scorecard to measure agency performance.

Admittedly, ratings are not indicative of how market forces might affect the price of a security, but maybe it's time for that to change. Expecting a risky mortgage to perform the same when home prices are dropping as it would in an appreciating market is completely unrealistic. Tying a portion of income to performance would change the agencies' motivation, forcing them to reevaluate their models and develop an unbiased rating process.

The hard part is implementation. It's questionable whether the SEC even has the statutory authority to modify how the agencies are compensated. If they don't have the power then Congress would need to grant it to them by amending the Credit Agency Reform Act or some other legislative reform, not an easy task. Given the current climate in Washington and the powerful influence of the rating agencies, my belief is that Congress will do very little to hold them accountable.

Mortgage Broker—Fixing the System

I was explaining to a friend the challenges we encountered working with mortgage brokers when he raised an interesting question. He asked whether the borrower was better served with or without brokers, given the problems they create. To this day, I still struggle with that question. In light of everything that has taken place, it's hard to specify the value they provide unless better forms of consumer protection are put into place.

While a good broker can be the best option for a homebuyer who needs a creative mortgage solution, this same type of borrower, the one with less than perfect credit, is also more vulnerable to manipulation. A middle ground, however, is within reach. In order for the system to provide sufficient consumer protections, reduce the ability to manipulate borrowers, and allow the broker to remain competitive, only a few modifications are required.

Fiduciary Duty—Start with the Money

The predatory lending bill in the House of Representatives requires the broker to act in the borrower's best interest. Since the measure has wide support in the Senate, it seems likely the final version will include such a provision. There are, however, a few concerns. First, how do you define best interest? Since the bill's language is somewhat nebulous in this area, it leaves room for interpretation and, inevitably, frivolous lawsuits. Second, creating a fiduciary duty doesn't completely address the problem's root cause. Admittedly, the broker should have a responsibility to the borrower, but unless the solution addresses the broker's motivation, it's only partially effective.

A recent movement that has gained popularity is the use of upfront brokers. A broker who operates in this manner agrees to take a specific fee that may be paid by the borrower, lender, or a combination of the two. The borrower and broker sign an agreement at loan application that details how much the broker will make on the transaction. Some states, like South Carolina, already require such an agreement to be signed for every mortgage application.

Developing this standard would put mortgage brokers on par with other real estate and financial service providers. When a homeowner sells a property, the listing agreement identifies how much the realtor will earn. When an investor buys stock through a broker, the commission is paid according to a designated schedule. Consumers who use CPAs or financial planners pay according to predetermined formulas. The mortgage broker's total compensation, however, can be a mystery until the final moments of the transaction. There are two reasons for this.

First, like any mortgage provider, brokers must disclose their fees on the good faith estimate (GFE). Since the GFE is just an estimate, there's no legal obligation to honor the quote. If a broker (or any mortgage professional) wants to increase fees at the last minute, the only thing that's required is a newly signed disclosure from the borrower. It's a deceptive practice that doesn't occur frequently but is allowable under the current system.

Second and more importantly, confusion occurs about how brokers disclose the yield-spread premium (YSP) on the GFE. Unlike the origination fee, which is identified by a dollar amount and percentage, the YSP is shown as a range, usually 0 to 3 percent. Since the borrower won't know the total YSP until shortly before closing, when the final settlement statement is developed, the broker's compensation remains a mystery until the last minute.

The use of an up-front agreement for brokered loans would create a significant protection for borrowers. Here's how it would work. Let's assume the two parties agree the broker will earn 150 basis points (1.5 percent of the loan amount) in total commissions. The money can come from the borrower, lender, or a combination of the two. Once a broker is bound by a set figure, consider what happens to his motivation. If the total fee can't change, there's no reason to treat a borrower unfairly. It would be nearly impossible to pull a bait and switch on a customer.

To be clear, I don't advocate limiting the amount or percentage a broker can earn. If a broker believes his service is worth more than the market average, he should be allowed to charge more. Of course, he'll need to set a higher standard for service to earn it, but that's how the free market is supposed to work.

Before opponents cry foul, let me address the obvious concern that it creates an unfair advantage for lenders. When borrowers shop for a mortgage it means comparing two items—interest rate and closing costs. Requiring an up-front agreement doesn't make the broker less competitive, just more transparent. It will require the broker to educate the borrower on the differences between brokers and lenders and how each of them makes money. Now there's a novel idea—an educated borrower. It appears the idea has started to gain traction. Washington Mutual announced in late 2007 that brokers would be required to inform borrowers how much money they'll be making for each loan. Unfortunately, a short time later, Washington Mutual announced it was shutting its wholesale division.

Since subprime has all but disappeared, the issue is not as relevant in today's market. The majority of loans are being written for borrowers who present a good credit risk. These are the same consumers who have options and will typically go with the provider that offers the lowest interest rate and fees. But that shouldn't be used as an excuse for not addressing the inherent flaws within the system. The day will come when credit standards begin to loosen, and when they do, the opportunity for abusive behavior will become more prevalent.

The bill approved in the House of Representatives proposes the use of a simple disclosure to identify the basic parameters of the mortgage—loan amount, loan-to-value, prepayment penalty, and other details. While out-of-pocket costs are included in the mix, the bill does not address the issue of an up-front agreement for brokers. Adding a paragraph that incorporates the language used in the South Carolina disclosure is the key to protecting consumers from unscrupulous brokers.

It's worth noting that Congress has been considering a ban on yield-spread premiums (YSP). While the bill in the House of Representatives prohibits brokers from earning YSP for loans above the APR threshold, as discussed earlier in this chapter, restricting its use in any form is unnecessary if an up-front agreement exists between the broker and the borrower. Any limitations on YSP would significantly hamper the broker's ability to compete in the marketplace.

If a borrower chooses not to pay a loan origination fee, whether he's working with a lender or a broker, he'll still pay for it in the form of a higher interest rate. While brokers must disclose this income as YSP, lenders have no disclosure requirement. They still earn the revenue from the higher interest rate when the loan is sold on the secondary market, only the borrower never knows about it.

Additionally, when a mortgage company advertises a *no-cost refinance*, it means the interest rate has to be raised so the premium earned from the higher rate can cover all the closing costs—proof that nothing is free in mortgage finance. Without the ability to earn a premium from the lender, brokers would be severely restricted in how they could structure loans for borrowers.

The next challenge is raising performance standards. This means focusing on two areas—knowledge, which is managed through licensing, and fraud prevention, which requires a creative, out-of-the-box solution.

Licensing and Accreditation

While many states have implemented licensing requirements for mortgage brokers, a national standard is long overdue. The question is whether licensing should apply to just brokers or to all loan originators. Some states exempt loan officers from licensing provided they work for a mortgage banker. The assumption is that lenders have a financial interest in the loan's performance and therefore have greater controls in place. Even though brokers were the primary instigators, it's clear that problems existed at every layer of the mortgage process. The solution is to hold all loan originators to the same standard, regardless of whom they work for.

Unfortunately, passing a licensing exam doesn't equate with competency. Most state tests are relatively easy, requiring candidates to answer multiple-choice questions on federal compliance, state licensing laws, and ethics. These are important subjects but they in no way assure the licensee is a proficient originator. Since the current proposal in the House of Representatives calls for a national licensing process similar to what many states already require, the bill doesn't go far enough to ensure that licensed loan originators will be competent.

The industry should consider raising its own standards and developing a system of accreditation. The Mortgage Bankers Association (MBA) has an accrediting process for mortgage lenders that leads to designations similar to those for accountants and financial planners, but there's nothing in place to certify the expertise of a loan officer.

In November 2007, the National Association of Mortgage Brokers (NAMB) introduced the Lending Integrity Seal of Approval (LISA) to identify mortgage brokers and loan officers who meet the industry's highest standards for knowledge, professionalism, ethics, and integrity. It's a positive step, but given the timing of the announcement, which coincided with the House of Representatives nearly passing a no-YSP provision in their lending bill, it looks more like a public relations strategy than a real effort at accreditation. Since the approval process takes only six weeks and the requirements are relatively simple to meet—hold a state license, complete a background check, attend educational courses—it scores points for style, but comes up short in the substance department.

The recent debacle has given brokers a reputation similar to used car salesmen. Although the bankers and brokers associations don't have a history of working together on issues, a collaborative effort to accredit loan originators would be a key step to rebuilding credibility for the industry. One day a CLO (Certified Loan Originator) designation could hold the same distinction as being a CPA or CFP. Allowing loan originators to earn a designation that recognizes their expertise not only improves their professionalism but also separates and identifies the strong performers from the average or weak ones.

Tackling Fraud—Thinking Outside the Box

With the recent upheaval in the real-estate market, the courts have shown a willingness to punish violators. In August 2006, a former American Home Mortgage Investment Corp. branch manager in Alaska was sentenced to two years in prison, fined $50,000, and ordered to pay $140,000 in restitution for wire fraud. He pleaded guilty to falsifying documents to secure stated income loans for customers while working for American Home Mortgage Investment Corp. and Countrywide Financial. This is the first known case in which an originator received jail time for increasing a borrower's income on the application, a common industry practice.

While advancements in technology have improved the industry's effort at detecting fraud, there's still a long way to go. By most estimates, lenders lose tens of millions of dollars each year as a result of fraudulent activities. For our purpose, the subject of fraud is addressed at the broker level. Even though borrowers, title companies, and other industry professionals contributed to the problem, they require a separate analysis and go beyond the scope of this book.

Though my company encountered fraud on a daily basis, there was little we could do to help other lenders. Without a mechanism for sharing the information with other mortgage companies, fraudulent brokers could easily move from one lender to another. The solution is to develop a national scoring system that tracks fraudulent activities for all loan originators.

Just as borrowers are scored based on their total credit profile, loan originators would earn fraud scores based on how they performed relative to certain measurements. If lenders took the raw data from each loan (without the borrower name and Social Security number) and submitted it to a central repository, a group of skilled statisticians could use the information to develop a scoring model.

In order for it to work, the system would require a gatekeeper. Whether the score was developed by a private company or through an industry-wide effort (coordinated by the Mortgage Bankers Association, for example), the system would be dependent on lenders providing the gatekeeper with data to develop a scoring model. Any lender that wanted access to the scores would pay a subscription for the service. Ideally, lenders that contributed data to the service would pay less for the subscription than lenders that didn't.

The key to making it work is to insure that the methodology is understandable to lenders and brokers. The reason goes back to motivation and behavior. If a loan officer realizes that his fraud score worsens if a large percentage of his deals are closed as stated income loans, he will be motivated not to take the easy way out. Conversely, if loan originators know certain behaviors will improve their score, they will be more inclined to act in that manner.

Once enough information has been compiled to create a reliable database, lenders will develop their own policies on how to use the scores. A loan officer who consistently received a poor fraud score would quickly find himself looking for a new career. A scoring system that potentially threatens an originator's livelihood becomes an enormous deterrent to fraudulent activity. If the use of fraud scores gained widespread acceptance among lenders, the agencies could eventually use them in rating securities.

Appraisers

Chapter 4 conducted a thorough examination of the appraisal process, detailing how a property's value can be manipulated. While today's problems resulted from a multitude of issues, overvalued appraisals caused significant economic damage. The solution to fixing the appraisal process comes with reducing the ability of brokers and realtors to influence an appraiser.

The best idea would be to completely overhaul the system and assign appraisers on a random or rotational basis, similar to the system used by the VA and thus eliminating the pressure to inflate property values. But the enormity of this task makes it difficult to envision, and a more realistic solution should be considered.

In the early days of the industry, lenders provided brokers with a list of approved appraisers. If a broker submitted a loan and the appraiser wasn't on the list, the deal was rejected outright. As brokers gained a larger share of the market, lenders loosened the requirement, believing it created an obstacle to attracting the broker's business. In time lenders went from having an approved list to identifying only appraisers they wouldn't accept, usually the worst violators. Letting brokers choose the appraiser may have reduced the barrier, but it also gave birth to a flawed process.

Of all the solutions discussed in this chapter, this one may be the easiest to implement: Reverting to the previous system would decrease the broker's ability to influence the property's value. The difference between having a list of approved and a list of unacceptable appraisers may seem minor, but it's actually significant. Since lenders develop the list, an appraiser has to apply to them in order to make the cut. Having to earn and keep a lender's confidence means thinking twice before giving in to the wishes of a manipulative broker. The threat of being removed from the list serves as a natural deterrent to massaging property values.

What are the negatives? If a broker moves a loan from one lender to another and the appraiser isn't approved by the second lender, a second appraisal must be ordered, which costs money and creates delays. This issue, although minor, will eventually fix itself. Once lenders develop their own lists, brokers will start choosing appraisers that are sanctioned by multiple lenders or encourage their preferred appraisers to get signed up with multiple companies.

Since lenders set their own appraisal policies, it's inconceivable that an industry-wide requirement could be mandated. Each lender would need to implement its own standards policy and develop a list of approved appraisers. Given that the total number of wholesale lenders has dropped by more than 60 percent over the last year, now is the best time to make this change. With brokers no longer carrying the influence they once did, if a few of the largest wholesale lenders announced the change, others would follow.

Of course, the underlying assumption is that lenders will act responsibly. Conventional wisdom dictates the risk of manipulating an appraised value far outweighs the reward for any lender. The financial upside from closing more loans is comparatively small compared to the repercussions of foreclosing on an overvalued property. In light of recent events, however, it seems that conventional wisdom may have taken a back seat to greed.

Andrew Cuomo, New York State's Attorney General, filed a lawsuit in November 2007 claiming eAppraisalIT, a subsidiary of First American Corporation and Washington Mutual, colluded to inflate appraised home values. Since eAppraisalIT provided over 250,000 appraisals to Washington Mutual during the course of their relationship, a guilty verdict would create an avalanche of consumer lawsuits.

Although we can't prevent a lender from acting irresponsibly if greed overtakes their thinking, Congress could prohibit mortgage bankers from having an ownership interest or participating in a joint venture with an appraisal company. This would require a provision in the national predatory lending law that lenders have no monetary or partnership interest in the appraisal company that conducts their work.

Lenders like Countrywide will argue that owning an appraisal services company allows them to accurately access a property's value, but the conflict of interest is too great. Objectivity only exists if there's distance between a lender and the appraiser. The SEC wouldn't allow an investment bank to own an agency that rates their securities. Why should mortgage lenders be permitted to own an appraisal company that determines property values for their mortgages? It's a conflict of interest that needs to be addressed.*

---

*Since this was originally written, Cuomo, along with Fannie Mae, Freddie Mac, and OFHEO, have struck an agreement on appraisal reform. The two most significant pieces of this agreement will prevent brokers from choosing the appraiser and prevent lenders from having an ownership interest in the company that does the appraisals.

Lending Guidelines—Meaningful Changes

Chapter 5 explained how the industry creatively structured loans to make them saleable. For all the faults associated with the business, changing the entire way it operates is not realistic. If a loan has problems, someone will devise a creative solution. The key is to address the areas that will protect the borrower from predatory practices while not restricting the availability of credit to consumers.

The next section identifies guidelines that need to be changed and proposes viable alternatives, which will be compared to the bill approved by the House of Representatives.

Prepayment Penalties

As a consumer, it's difficult to see the value in a prepayment penalty. When given a choice between a loan with a prepayment penalty and a loan without one, the natural inclination would be to choose the loan with no penalty. Unfortunately, the subprime industry failed on two fronts. It used prepayment penalties excessively and neglected to consistently give consumers other options.

When used correctly, prepayment penalties should allow for a trade-off. Any quote that includes a prepayment penalty should also include a corresponding alternative with no penalty. If a borrower chooses a mortgage with a prepayment penalty, he benefits from a lower interest rate, while opting out of a prepayment penalty means paying a higher interest rate.

The lending industry has argued that a total elimination of prepayment penalties will result in the reduction of credit availability to the consumer. I believe this is false. Each of our investor's rate sheets had pricing options that ran the gamut from loans with no prepayment penalties to those with penalties for five years. Kellner could offer the same loan programs in every state; the only difference between them was the interest rate.

Over the last eight years, several states have addressed the issue with proposals ranging from total elimination of prepayment penalties to various restrictions on their use. When used fairly, prepayment penalties can serve their intended purpose without creating an unnecessary hardship for the borrower. To accomplish both objectives requires a national prepayment policy that includes the following components:

95 Percent Maximum Loan-to-Value (LTV). Prepayment penalties shouldn't be allowed for mortgages exceeding 95 percent LTV. If a borrower purchased with no money down or refinanced the full value of a property, the likelihood that the home will sell or the loan will refinance in the near term is small. Prepayment penalties for loans above 95 percent create a hardship for borrowers who have to move unexpectedly. An alternative solution is to allow a "soft" prepayment penalty for loans above 95 percent LTV. This penalty would only apply if the borrower refinanced the mortgage and it would not apply if the home was sold. At present, the bill in the House of Representatives does not address prepayment penalties relative to LTV.

3 Percent Maximum Prepayment Penalty. A 5 percent prepayment penalty does wonders for a lender's profitability, but it creates an unnecessary burden for consumers. By standardizing penalties using a step-down method, 3 percent for the first year, 2 percent for the second year, and 1 percent for the third year, the secondary market will get its deterrent and consumers won't be excessively penalized. The 3/2/1 formula is the fairest approach for both groups. It allows the industry to retain the maximum benefit during the first year, when it needs it most, and less for the following years. This is identical to the current proposal in the House of Representatives.

Adjustable Rate Mortgages (ARMs). Prepayment penalties on adjustable rate mortgages should be limited in duration until the first rate adjustment occurs. If a borrower has a two-year adjustable rate mortgage, the prepayment penalty should be limited to 24 months. Whether a loan is fixed or adjustable, all penalties should be capped at three years. The proposal in the House is more favorable to the industry, allowing penalties to go three months beyond the initial adjustment.

ARMs—Changing the Methodology

The steady rise we've seen in mortgage delinquencies is due, in part, to the widespread use of ARMs. To understand how this type of loan impacted the borrower's ability to pay, consider the numbers in Table 7.1. It summarizes the debt-to-income (DTI) ratios for all full-documentation ARM loans my company closed from 2000 to 2005. DTI is calculated by adding together the monthly mortgage payment (including property tax and homeowners insurance), plus installment and revolving debt, and dividing that figure by gross monthly income. Most subprime lenders allowed maximum DTI ratios of 50 to 55 percent.

The first column is a range of DTI ratios in 5 percent increments, and the second column represents the percentage of loans that fit into each category. The second column shows that almost 90 percent of borrowers had DTI ratios of 50 percent or less. The third column estimates what the DTI ratios would be for the same loans once the interest rate adjusts (either two or three years into the

Table 7.1 Debt-to-Income (DTI) Ratios (ARM Loans Only)

DTI Ratios (at closing)	% of All Loans (at 1st adjustment)	% of All Loans
Less than 40%	28%	4%
41–45%	30%	12%
46–50%	29%	24%
51–55%	13%	31%
55%+	0%	29%

future). Calculating this estimate requires making two assumptions: First, borrower's income and debt levels remain constant, and second, the interest rate increases by 3 percent, the maximum allowed at the first adjustment period. This scenario is very likely for borrowers who obtained an ARM after 2003 when the Fed started raising interest rates.

The impact of the rate increase is profound. Most borrowers started with DTI ratios that were already high. Once the interest rate adjusts, the ratios increase an average of 7 percent. While most borrowers had DTI ratios less than 50 percent at the initial closing, column three shows that six out of ten borrowers would have DTI ratios greater than 50 percent after the interest rate adjusted. This means the majority of these borrowers would no longer qualify for financing.

Consider how this problem becomes magnified when applied to the stated income loan. We already know that from 2002 to 2006 the percentage of subprime borrowers using stated income loans was steadily rising. We don't know the DTI ratios since income was never disclosed, but a basic assumption can be made that a large percentage wouldn't have qualified had they been required to prove income. This means their initial DTI ratios would be higher than the levels shown for the borrowers in column two, and the adjusted DTI ratios in column three would also be higher. It adds up to an enormously disproportionate amount of borrowers who can't afford their mortgage payments.

The solution is to qualify borrowers at the time of loan application using the fully indexed rate. Instead of using the low start rate that ARMs are known for, the lender would qualify the borrower as if the ARM were making its first interest rate adjustment. This is calculated by adding the loan's predetermined margin to a specific monetary index. The majority of subprime loans used the 6-month LIBOR (London Interbank Offered Rate) as the index of choice. Historically, the fully indexed rate is 2 to 2.25 percent higher than the start rate at the time of the loan's closing. If this policy had existed a few years ago, many of the borrowers currently in default would have been denied a mortgage. This approach mirrors the current proposal in the House of Representatives.

Escrow Accounts

Of all the poor decisions the industry made, not requiring subprime borrowers to use escrow accounts for collecting property tax and insurance payments ranks near the top. Many "A" credit borrowers choose to set up escrow accounts for the convenience of not paying a large bill at year-end. Others prefer to manage the process themselves, believing it's better to earn interest on the money and control their funds. Since many subprime borrowers live paycheck-to-paycheck, expecting them to save money each month to pay for taxes and insurance is unrealistic. These borrowers needed the discipline an escrow account provided, but the industry never made it mandatory.

The solution is simple. If a borrower is classified as high-risk, escrow accounts should be mandatory. The current bill in the House of Representatives establishes a long list of provisions that trigger an escrow account requirement, ranging from the interest rate to the loan-to-value percentage. I'll spare you the details, but suffice it to say that most of the requirements are well thought out. The only item that's missing is an exception for borrowers who have more than six months of cash reserves to cover PITI (principal, interest, taxes, and insurance) after closing. If substantial reserves are in place, the need for an escrow account is not as critical.

Mandatory Counseling

One of the more unique products offered by the lending industry is the reverse mortgage, which enables seniors to tap into their home equity without having to make any payments. Part of the approval process requires all seniors to attend a HUD-approved counseling session. The same logic should apply to the subprime borrower. Attending a simple one-hour HUD-approved counseling session that provides basic information about the mortgage process would go a long way toward protecting the borrower.

A borrower armed with knowledge becomes a deterrent to abusive behavior. The reason we don't hear stories about seniors getting bad deals for reverse mortgages is due, in part, to the education they receive. Once the appropriate safeguards are in place, the industry will start to rid itself of the worst violators. The House of Representatives has included counseling as part of its final bill by establishing an Office of Housing Counseling through the Department of Housing and Urban Development.

Taking the Cheat Out of the Liar

The basic premise for the stated income loan has changed drastically over the last 20 years. Helping the high FICO score, a self-employed borrower who possesses a down payment is a far cry from lending money to anyone with a pulse. Since the bill in the House effectively calls for the elimination of the stated income loan, it's conceivable the final version will do the same. The industry drastically overshot the mark with the stated income loan and calling for its total elimination might appear to be a wise decision, but it's a shortsighted policy. We only need to look at the history of this product to understand why.

For years prior to the subprime debacle, the lending industry offered stated or limited documentation loans without any significant problems. Why? It managed the risk appropriately. As we look back on the actions of the industry these last few years, we now understand that the industry forgot it was in the risk business. That was a mistake of monumental proportions, but it doesn't mean the basic principles that originally justified the use of stated income loans have changed.

A borrower with a 750 credit score who can't prove his income is still a better credit risk than someone with a 600 score and three jobs. Why? It goes back to a credit score's ability to predict performance. A borrower with a 750 score has a strong record of making timely payments. The discipline that's required to earn this score tells us there's a very small chance he's going to default, even if he isn't employed. The 600 score borrower hasn't shown this level of discipline. That doesn't mean we arbitrarily draw lines in the sand and say those with scores greater than "x" can qualify and others can't. It means borrowers at any credit grade can qualify for a stated income loan provided all the credit and risk factors are managed appropriately.

For all the complexity of the loan business, it's not rocket science. If a borrower with a 600 score wants a stated income loan, he needs to have more skin in the game than someone with a 750 score. While market forces should be allowed to dictate what's the appropriate level of down payment for each credit grade, a significant cash reserve requirement would go a long way toward managing the risk for this product.

The biggest flaw of the stated income loan, especially at the lower end of the credit spectrum, was the lack of cash reserves after closing. Therefore, the lending law should include a significant cash reserve requirement for all loans in which the lender is unable to verify a borrower's income. It should include the following provisions:

- Borrowers with credit scores above 660 should meet a minimum nine-month cash reserve requirement (principal, interest, taxes, and insurance) after all closing costs are accounted for.
- Borrowers below 660 should meet a 12-month cash reserve requirement.

In all cases, borrowers should have to show proof of funds for a minimum of two months. Most subprime loans had no such seasoning requirement, which meant the funds were borrowed from relatives at the last minute, put into a bank account, and then verified. Since most home purchase transactions take 60 days or less to conduct, there's no need to extend the seasoning requirement beyond that.

If greater cash reserves had been required, many borrowers who financed with marginal credit and no proof of income would have been declined. The stated or limited documentation loan works only if borrowers who can't prove income have cash reserves to fall back on and the industry prices the loan for the additional risk. When the interest rate for a stated income loan started to mirror the interest rate for a full documentation loan, it was the beginning of the end.

Despite all my posturing about not instilling limitations on the availability of credit, there's one area that warrants consideration. A subprime wage earner—someone who earns a fixed wage— shouldn't be allowed to qualify for a stated income loan. If a borrower's income doesn't fluctuate, he should be required to prove it in order to qualify. The stated income program was originally designed to serve the needs of the self-employed borrower and that's where it should stay.

The Current Crisis

The next two years may very well be the worst in the history of the U.S. housing market. Friends and colleagues usually regard me as an optimist but, unfortunately, I've witnessed the gluttony that infested the lending industry and I'm afraid there is no silver lining to the dark cloud that's over the industry now. The questions of concern going forward should be: Just how bad will this crisis get, at what point will the market stabilize, and is there anything that can or should be done to reduce the fallout?

Most experts predict foreclosures will peak sometime in 2009, with the total number reaching two million. The markets that experienced the highest levels of home appreciation, such as Las Vegas and Miami, are projected to see home values drop by as much as 40 to 50 percent (from peak to trough). While areas that never experienced a huge run-up in home prices aren't projecting a drop in the median price of homes, there are two factors that could be wild cards in the housing equation.

The first one is Pay-Option ARMs. A Pay-Option ARM is different from a traditional subprime ARM in several ways. While both have low start rates, the Pay-Option ARM often has ultralow start rates, sometimes as low as 1 percent. As the name implies, the Pay-Option ARM allows borrowers to choose from one of several different payment options. It's often referred to as a neg-am (negative amortization) loan because the principal loan balance will increase if the borrower makes only the minimum payment. This product also differs in that each loan comes with a maximum negative allowance. This means that when the principal loan balance reaches a certain level, typically between 110 to 125 percent of the original loan amount depending on how the mortgage was structured, the payment increases. Unlike a traditional ARM, when a Pay-Option ARM adjusts, the payment can increase by as much as two to three times the original amount.

The product was originally conceived as a loan option for astute investors who wanted to use their money for something other than paying mortgage principal. As home prices soared, it morphed into the only method available for hundreds of thousands of borrowers to qualify in overpriced markets like California. The numbers paint a troubling picture.

An industry veteran with 20 years experience in mortgage lending, who asked not to be identified, worked for one of the largest and most aggressive Pay-Option ARM lenders in California. These are the figures he shared with respect to his former employer's book of business. Nearly three-fourths of the borrowers with Pay-Option ARMs made the minimum monthly payment. Over 80 percent of the loans during the last few years were written as stated income. The majority of all Pay-Option ARMs have second mortgages behind them (piggybacks), which puts the combined loan-to-value percentage at or above 90 percent. Even if the figures for all Pay-Option ARMs are only half as bad as he claims, it means there is a second wave to this mortgage crisis.

Credit Suisse recently published a report that broke down the volume of mortgage ARM resets by month and product type over the next seven years. It shows that Pay-Option ARMs will begin to significantly reset in late 2009 and peak in 2011. There are more than $250 billion worth of Pay-Option ARMs scheduled to reset by 2011. In all likelihood, values will have dropped in overvalued markets by that time, making it impossible to refinance. When you consider all of these factors, the issues with Pay-Option ARMs could easily dwarf the subprime implosion. In some ways, it's already happening. It just has not yet received widespread media attention.

In the introduction to this book, I mentioned that the mortgage crisis is not currently contained to the subprime arena. Nowhere is this more evident than in the world of Alt-A mortgages, of which Pay-Option ARMs are a subset. In late February 2008, Mike "Mish" Shedlock of Global Economic Trend Analysis, one of the most widely read economic blogs in the United States, posted a screen shot forwarded to him by a colleague from a specific Washington Mutual Alt-A mortgage pool known as WMALT 2007-0C1. The screen breaks down the pool of mortgages into the typical categories, including delinquencies. Here are some of the highlights. The average FICO score is 705—not spectacular but respectable by most standards. We don't know for certain if these are Pay-Option ARMs, but there's a good chance most of them are with over 60 percent of the entire pool coming from California and Florida. Most of the loans were written with little to no money down and almost 90 percent of the pool is comprised of stated income loans.

The chart breaks down performance by month, starting with July 2007. Keep in mind that the pool has been in existence for only nine months at the time this book was going to press. In that short period, this pool is already showing a foreclosure rate of 13.17 percent. Add REOs (real estate owned by the lender) into the mix and the figure goes to 15 percent. Even the vintage 2006 subprime pools didn't default as quickly.

A look at the details shows that nearly 93 percent of the pool was rated AAA, yet almost 15 percent of the entire pool is in foreclosure or REO after nine months. If there was ever a doubt about the ineptitude of the rating agencies, this pool of loans is proof.

The numbers seem to indicate that borrowers may be walking away when they are only 30 or 60 days delinquent, not even waiting for foreclosure. In December 2007, the 90 days delinquent category stood at 3.79 percent. Even if every one of these delinquencies became a foreclosure, the figure should only double to 7.58 percent in January. Instead, the foreclosure figure jumped to 13.17 percent. These figures suggest the recent phenomenon known as jingle mail—when borrowers mail their keys back to their lenders before going to foreclosure—is alive and well.

The second wild card is credit availability. While a national lending bill will have some impact in this area, my concern comes from watching the mortgage industry during these last six months. Since the middle of 2007, lenders have eliminated or restricted program guidelines as a result of rising delinquencies. As losses rise throughout 2008, and there is little reason to think they won't, this could lead to a disturbing trend.

The concern is that a pattern will develop that progressively gets worse as time goes along. A rise in mortgage defaults will lead to increased losses for investors, causing lenders to pull back even further on guidelines. The reduction in credit means more borrowers won't qualify. When they don't buy homes, inventories will rise, forcing more borrowers into default. Since there are two million homeowners with subprime ARMs set to adjust in the next 24 months (the majority occurring in the next year), there is no historical reference, short of the Great Depression, for what's about to happen in the national housing market. To make matters worse, about the time we've cleared through the inventory of foreclosures because of subprime ARMs, the Pay-Option ARMs will begin to reset. The bottom won't come until prices have dropped far enough so that the housing supply can stabilize. Since the current national housing supply is nearly double what it should be (a six-month supply is considered normal), it's impossible to predict when the market will achieve equilibrium.

I have no pearls of wisdom on how to prevent the large number of pending foreclosures. The Bush administration's plan to freeze

ARM rates will help some borrowers, but the overall impact is going to be minimal. Since the program is voluntary, it will work only if the Wall Street firms sell the idea to the investment funds that hold the mortgage-backed securities—an unlikely scenario. Additionally, tranche warfare is going to create barriers that limit mortgage servicers from making changes.

The business of mortgage securitization not only helped finance a multitude of unqualified borrowers, it's now preventing servicers from modifying their loans. When the problem reaches critical mass, don't be surprised if "mortgage securitization giveth and mortgage securitization taketh away" becomes the industry's motto.

Perhaps what should be addressed are the ramifications of a bailout. Any plan that helps distressed borrowers will come at the expense of taxpayers or investors who purchased the securities. Some of the groups who invested in subprime securities include cities, counties, and even school boards. A state-run fund in Florida has declined so drastically that officials had to freeze it, preventing some school districts from paying their teachers. It's hard to justify helping borrowers who knew what they were getting into when basic governmental services are suffering as a result of their delinquencies.

Even a plan to freeze rates has consequences. Somewhere in the splicing and dicing of a mortgage-backed security, an investor is entitled to an increased revenue stream when the ARM rates start to adjust. Admittedly, there is a threat of default which could lead to greater losses for the investor, but why should anybody, investor or taxpayer, foot the bill for borrowers who are in over their heads? When will borrowers be held accountable for their actions?

In the midst of this mess, we shouldn't forget that this country suffers from an affordability crisis. Since income has not kept pace with the cost of housing over the last ten years, the dream of homeownership will remain just that, a dream, for many people, especially those who live in the most overinflated markets. Perhaps the only solution is to let the cards fall where they may and allow the natural forces of the market to correct themselves. It may not be the most popular sentiment and the economic implications would be staggering, but given the depth and severity of this problem, there may not be any other choice.

Final Thoughts

When people used to ask me what I did for a living, the answer was never, "I'm a mortgage lender." Instead I would tell them, "I'm a subprime lender." I knew the system was less than perfect, but it really felt like we in the subprime business made a positive difference in people's lives. Perhaps we deluded ourselves to a certain degree, but since our loans performed well relative to our investors' expectations, it was easy to think that way.

Although my gut still tells me we did more good than harm, I also realize that at some point logic and risk-based thinking gave way to our desire to keep growing the business. I can point fingers at a lot of different groups, but at the end of the day we ourselves still pulled the trigger on every deal. We decided whether a borrower was a good credit risk and we funded the loan using our own money. No one else made that final decision. With such power comes responsibility, and like it or not, I can't sit here without putting some of the blame back onto myself.

It's entirely possible that I was somewhat naïve. Until Kellner was formed, my world seemed fairly black and white. I viewed most things as being right or wrong, and seldom was there an in-between. What surprised me about subprime lending was that there were very few absolutes. Lending money to people with bad credit means living in a world of gray. The longer I stayed there, especially in light of the changes that took place in the market, the more difficult it became to distinguish what constituted a good credit risk.

Johnny Cutter, our borrower from Chapter 1, taught me an interesting lesson. When I spoke to him one last time shortly before he moved out of the house, he thanked me for giving him a way out. His comment took me by surprise. Since I had just convinced him to hand over the keys to his home, I wasn't exactly feeling like a philanthropist. I knew that most subprime lenders, especially the larger companies, wouldn't have treated him as well given the circumstances, but the process still left me with a knot in my stomach.

What Johnny's loan taught me was to trust my instincts. I had deluded myself into thinking that somehow our decision to write more loans, make less money, and take on more risk would work itself out. My gut kept telling me something had to give since the business model was making less sense every day, but I couldn't bring myself to do anything about it. It took my having to confront one of our borrowers, who never should've been given a loan in the first place, to realize I knew the answer all along.

GLOSSARY

automated valuation models (AVMs)   Computer programs that rely on statistical models to provide value estimates for residential real estate.

basis points (BPS)   A unit that is equal to 1/100th of 1 percent. Basis points are commonly used for calculating changes in interest rates.

broker price opinion (BPO)   An estimate of a residential property's probable selling price based on the selling prices of comparable properties in the area. Often used by a mortgage servicer as an alternative to a full property appraisal.

credit score   A measure of a person's credit risk, calculated using the information from their credit report.

collateralized debt obligation (CDO)   A type of asset-backed security that divides the credit risk among different tranches (sections) of a securitized mortgage package.

debt-to-income (DTI)   The percentage of a borrower's monthly gross income that goes toward paying debts.

government sponsored entities (GSEs)   The generic terminology used to describe the loan companies known as Fannie Mae or Freddie Mac.

loan-to-value (LTV)   A calculation that expresses the amount of the first mortgage lien as a percentage of the appraised value or purchase price, whichever is lower.

mortgage-backed security (MBS) An investment product in which thousands of mortgage loans are bundled together and sold as bonds.

mortgage insurance (MI) An insurance policy bought by the borrower to protect the lender against default of loans greater than 80 percent loan-to-value (LTV).

piggyback mortgage A second mortgage taken out simultaneously with the first in order to provide funds for a down payment.

prepayment penalty A specified percentage charged by the lender when all or part of a mortgage principal amount is repaid before a certain time period.

tranche A French word that means slice, section, or series. It refers to one of several related securitized bonds offered as part of the same deal.

RESOURCES

Abelson, Alan. "After the Greenspan Put . . ." *Barron's*, August 13, 2007.

Cariaga, Vance. "Credit Agencies, Banks, Buyers Share Blame for Subprime Mess." *Investor's Business Daily*, August 16, 2007.

Chomsisengphet, Souphala and Anthony Pennington-Cross. "The Evolution of the Subprime Mortgage Market." *Federal Reserve Bank of St. Louis Review*, January/February 2006.

Eggert, Kurt. "Role of Securitization in Subprime Mortgage Market Turmoil." Testimony to the Committee on Senate Banking, Housing and Urban Affairs Subcommittee on Securities, Insurance and Investments, April 17, 2007.

Hudson, Michael. "How Wall Street Stoked the Mortgage Meltdown." RealEstateJournal.com, August 16, 2007. http://www.realestatejournal.com/buysell/mortgages/20070628-hudson.html.

Levitt, Steven, and Stephen Dubner. *Freakonomics: A Rogue Economist Explores the Hidden Side of Everything*. New York: HarperCollins, 2005.

Mauldin, John. "Back to the 1998 Crisis, Subprime to Impact for a Long Time." The Market Oracle, August 11, 2007. http://www.marketoracle.co.uk/Article1792.html.

Mauldin, John. "The Ongoing Impact of the Housing Market." Outside the Box, August 24, 2007. http://www.investorsinsight.com/otb_va_print.aspx.

Roberts, Ralph, and Rachel Dollar. *Protect Yourself from Real Estate and Mortgage Fraud*. New York: Kaplan Publishing, 2007.

Rosner, Joshua. "Stopping the Subprime Crisis." *Wall Street Journal*, July 25, 2007.

Tomlinson, Richard, and David Evans. "A Ratings Charade?" *Seattle Times*, August 12, 2007. http://seattletimes.nwsource.com/html/businesstechnology/200383227_subprime12.html.